PRAISE FO
BECOMING AN IDEA

D1108854

"Bold, empowering, transparent, and
anyone with an idea locked away in their head and heart as
a startup, ministry, or private passion. As John unfolds the
concept of unlocking the idea, the reader will find means and
ways of bringing it to full life!"
     - Dr. Andrew K. Fox, Founder, Cultural Clarity

As a father of 4 children, I am consistently reminded of the
creative capacity instilled within each human. Yet, as we
"grow up" and "mature", the more we tend to slide into a
monotonous day-to-day life that is both boring and uninspiring.
Where does that imagination and creativity go? John Voelz has
a unique ability to re-awaken the creative imagination that is
still deep within each of our cores, but often necessitates an
intentional resurrection. This book will do just that!
     - Dr. Heath Hollensbe, Author, Podcaster,
     and Public Speaker

In John Voelz' "Becoming an Idea Mentalist," I have found
myself revisiting key points and thoughts again and again. I
have found inspiration once again and hear John's voice in my
ear as I learn to push the edges on "being comfortable" and
pursuing new life endeavors.

For myself, this is not a quick read or a have-it-all-figured-out-
now-type-self-help-guru-book. It is like a fine wine that you
need to take hold of, savor, consider the elements, and taste.
Use this book for inspiration and deep thought, a bit of humor,
as well as reflection.

For certain, as you read, new ideas, new thoughts, new
reflections will come. Sit with them, ponder, and stop being

satisfied with the "status quo." Now more than ever, this book is relevant not only to me but to society as a whole.

- **David McKay,** Author and Owner of McKay Photography Academy

In reading John's book, Becoming an Idea Mentalist, I learned practical and provocative ways to mine for creativity by capturing truly unique thoughts from the collective and connected rather than sheer individual will power. This book illustrates the adage, "No one of us is as smart as all of us!" So, here's a great idea... Read this book, learn a few new words (like Moothanasia!) and see what happens!

- **Dan Perkins**, Head Coach at FNSH Endurance Coaching, Executive Leadership Coach

"This book gives you a framework for creativity.... plus mad springs and a killer mat so you can do those kick-ass flips you've been dreaming of."

- **Pierre du Plessis**, Artist, Author, and TedX Speaker

John Voelz' Becoming an Idea Mentalist is essential reading for many of us stuck living two-dimensional lives. John masterfully shines the light on how we can practically experience a three-dimensional life instead: one in which we get past our routines and limiting fears and step into tasting, seeing, hearing, feeling, and smelling the beauty and joy of life. Being an Idea Mentalist is the antidote to living a "same ol' same ol' " life and the catalyst to unlocking the creative contributors we all are made to be.

- **Vineet Rajan**, Co-Founder & CEO at Paraclete

Becoming an Idea Mentalist disrupts systems stuck in the status quo. As I read it, what immediately came to mind was the Oakland A's 20-game win streak, the 49ers' dominance in the 80's, and the Warriors' rise to basketball dynasty. John Voelz says, *"You must be aware that somewhere out there, someone is tweaking ideas and inventing new ways of doing things that will change the world."*

MoneyBall, the West Coast offense, and Small-Ball all came from innovative Idea Mentalists. Now anyone can benefit from this masterful playbook that empowers individuals, teams, organizations, or businesses that want to change the game.

    - **Jon Talbert**, Chaplain to the Oakland A's

I've been a little outside the proverbial box all my life, pushing boundaries, inviting different angles, and collaborating with creatives. John Voelz makes me look like a novice; and I love it. This is your opportunity to learn his trade secrets for creative excellence, practices for refreshing viewpoints, and tenets for fostering new direction. Becoming an Idea Mentalist is a roadmap for breaking rules in all the right ways. Don't miss out on your opportunity.

    - **Dr. Becky Veydt**, Consultant, Coach at Invite
      Family Business Consulting

Every organization needs to innovate. Few, however, know where to begin. Drawing from his decades as a creative leader, and using stories from his career and personal experiences, John Voelz gives readers simple but powerful ideas that they can use to build an organization committed to innovation. -

    - **Dave Wahlstedt**, Director: Ugandan Shoe Trees

BECOMING AN IDEA MENTALIST

THE UNUSUAL PERSPECTIVES, PRACTICES AND RITUALS OF IDEA PEOPLE

JOHN VOELZ

FOREWORD BY
DR. DAVID MCDONALD

FOSSORES PUBLISHING
JACKSON, MI

Becoming an Idea Mentalist: The Unusual Perspectives, Practices and Rituals of Idea People

Foreword by Dr. David McDonald
Cover design by John Voelz
Cover logo by Karysa Trombley
Layout and book design by Melissa Evans

FOSSORES PUBLISHING
505 Wildwood Avenue
Jackson, Michigan 49201
www.fossoreschapterhouse.com

This book is dedicated to Tahni who is an Idea Mentalist, encourages me to act on my crazy ideas, tolerates me when I am consumed by them, celebrates with me when the ideas are triumphant, cackles with me when the ideas prove the naysayers wrong, mourns with me when they don't work out as planned, speaks wisdom in my direction when I am out of my freaking mind, and is always there with me when I don't listen to that wisdom.

TABLE OF CONTENTS

FOREWORD..……….010

PROLOGUE...012

PART ONE
The Mind of an Idea Mentalist.................................017

CHAPTER ONE
In the Beginning...018

CHAPTER TWO
Creation..028

CHAPTER THREE
Philosophy of an Idea Mentalist.............................036

CHAPTER FOUR
Philosophy of an Idea Mentalist: Part Deux
(Who says I can't have a Part Deux?)....................070

PART TWO
The Habits of a Mentalist.......................................105

CHAPTER FIVE
Everything New..106

CHAPTER SIX
Give Me My Space...146

CHAPTER SEVEN
It's a Play Thing..168

CHAPTER EIGHT
Innovation Training..198

CHAPTER NINE
A Whole New World. Or…A World Reset...................…..238

CHAPTER TEN
Where Do We Go From Here?.................................…..260

EPILOGUE..274

FOREWORD

Laughter makes the work better. So does caffeine. And sunshine in a convertible. And music. And a walk outside in the snow. And lunch. And getting off topic. And talking too loud. And refusing to totally play by the rules.

I learned these important truths about work from my friend John, the original Idea Mentalist. John (or Jvo, as we all called him), knows a thousand ways to make work better—meaning, of a superior quality, and also of a superior experience. He knows that well-behaved people need to explore their mischievous impulses. He knows that rebels need constraints so their passions have something against which to rail. He knows that genius-level intellects need new and interesting problems to solve. He knows that hammers need nails, chaos needs order, and every now and then church ladies need to put on some slutty shoes.

Jvo has taught himself the secret to indefatigable creativity, and has compiled all he knows in this helpful little book so you don't have to beg him for ideas. You can have your own ideas, and play with them, too. You can decide to make your work better, to make your life better, to elevate the ordinary into the extraordinary and turn the mundane into magic. But it all starts with you—you're the one who has to decide, now, that you're done doing the same damn things all the damn time.

Take a risk.
Trust your gut.
Swing for the fences.

Because your best ideas have yet to be formed.

This book will fill you with seeds that will grow into great ideas, great experiences, and great work. You'll read it and re-read it often, finding more hidden gems with each return. So take it, use it, relish it, and most importantly...

Enjoy!

Dr. David McDonald
Founder: Fossores Chapter House

PROLOGUE

I started writing this book in the spring of 2019. Casually. On vacation.

For most of my adult life, people have been asking me how I come up with ideas. What resources are there for idea generation? Does it just happen? Is there some process you go through? Do you think you were just gifted with the ability to come up with new innovations?

For the longest time, I thought these were funny questions. Odd. Sometimes, I thought the questions were flattery, or, at least, people just being kind. When I was a young adult, I thought, "Duh. You just come up with them."

Somewhere along the line, I realized I have a *knack* for ideas. There is a part of me that feels it is a gift of some kind, but I don't believe that's the whole of it. As I sat one day and pondered what has happened in my journey that may have *prepared* me to easily generate ideas, I came up with a long list.

I shared that list with a few friends. I shared the list in parts here and there at conferences and in private coaching sessions. It seemed fitting to gather all my thoughts as best I could and put them in book form.

This isn't my first book. I've self-published a few and I've had some published by professional publishing houses. But I almost didn't start writing at all. I was offered a book deal because of an idea I had once upon a time that garnered national attention. I almost turned that offer down. I had grown tired of people on social media, at conferences, and in books claiming to be experts and tooting their horns. I didn't want to be lumped in with them.

One day, soon after the offer, I was visiting with my mentor. Len has been an editor in my life—not a book editor, but someone I have invited into my life to call me on my BS and help me become the best possible version of me. I told Len I wasn't going to accept that book offer and told him why. I'll never forget the pregnant pause, the turn in his chair, the look he gave me, and the words, "Shame on you." He wasn't really *shaming* me. He followed it up with, "Are you kidding me?"

He went on to encourage me by saying I had something to offer the world. He told me not to look at my words as bragging. Instead, I should look at my words as something that just might help someone somewhere. He was so right. I had become a victim of my own false humility and it was holding me back from my own progress and what I now understand as my responsibility to others as we lock arms on this human plane.

I share what I know. You share what you know. We all learn together.

I celebrate the things I've learned and keep learning that help to keep me sharp when it comes to generating ideas. I believe in what I've written here. I really hope it helps you. Do what you want with it. If you disagree, that's okay. If you think I've written something foolish, so be it. But, whatever you do, grapple with it.

I think we all have something to offer the world. Those offerings start with *ideas.* You have ideas locked inside you that are clawing to get out. Those ideas need nurturing, stirring, a right mindset, and a ripe environment for them to surface.

A ripe environment. Let's talk about that for a spell . . .

It's been said, "Necessity is the mother of invention." No one knows where that proverb originated. Variations of the same sentiment show up throughout literature spanning as far back as 375 BC with Plato.

However, while necessity may certainly stir ideas in all of us, it doesn't happen for everyone. Necessity doesn't birth the same number of ideas in everyone, nor do the ideas come as easily or as frequently for everyone. Some find themselves in crisis and have absolutely no clue how they will move forward and survive.

Necessity doesn't *necessarily* propel everyone to come up with *good* ideas. However, I absolutely believe with every stitch of my being that an Idea Mentalist (which we'll define throughout this entire book) is *best positioned* to generate ideas when necessity arises.

Three monumental changes happened in my life between starting this book and finishing it. These changes commanded and begged for new ideas. You and I have one of the things in common.

I got fired and subsequently sun-setted a thirty-year career.

My wife and I invested everything we had into starting a restaurant that opened on March 9, 2020.

A worldwide pandemic changed us forever.

I won't tell the story of my firing, though I will reference it here and there because I think it's important to know what ultimately *led* to my firing. Hint: In part, it has something to do with *ideas.*

Opening the restaurant was a dream come true and a nightmare realized at the same time. We did a soft-open on March 2, 2020, and a full-blown Grand Opening on March 9. The first week was amazing. We said to ourselves, "Look at our dream and our great ideas at work." On March 15, we held our first staff meeting and let our entire staff go. COVID-19 is the devil.

If ever there was a time in our lives where ideas were paramount, it was 2020. I'm thankful for my family's ability to generate ideas during crises. The ideas (along with an incredibly supportive and generous community) saved us, and I believe positioned us for greater things.

But this book is not simply about innovation when it's necessary.

It's about innovation when things are going *smoothly*.

It's about innovation when things are *stale*.

When it's *status quo*.

When people around you say it *isn't* necessary.

Because you want to *make things better*.

Because you want to *invest in people*.

Because you want to get *ahead* of change.

Because you *never want to be caught unawares* without an idea in your pocket.

Because you are *creative*.

Because of *your legacy*.

It's about ideas for the sake of ideas.

I finished this book in early 2022. There has never been a time in my life where I think this book is more relevant—not because of what we've come through. Because of what we're still in. Because of where we're going.

I hope you enjoy reading it.

John

PART ONE

THE MIND OF AN IDEA MENTALIST

CHAPTER ONE
IN THE BEGINNING

"The best way to have a good idea is to have a lot of ideas."
—Linus Pauling

Ideas Are a Precious Commodity

My mother-in-law called me an *experience junkie* in my
twenties and warned me to not go looking for an *experience*
outside of her daughter. Good advice.

But, I don't see myself as a junkie.

I think of experience junkies as the type of people who seek
out new thrills simply for the sake of the experience—throwing
caution to the wind. Without fear. Without care about the
consequences. Living off of adrenaline. Always needing a new
high and not being comfortable with downtime.

That's not me.

I know why my mother-in-law labeled me this way. My
favorite restaurant is the one I haven't been to yet. I don't like
trying to recreate experiences. I love stretching and growing. I
get bored in the same ol' same ol' world. I'm curious.

I love new ideas.

New ideas come from new experiences. The ones we create.
The ones we happen upon. The ones we plan for but still get
surprised by.

So, this book is going to talk a lot about experiences. You
need them. They are essential and fabric to becoming an Idea
Mentalist.

Each experience I have is an opportunity to learn. I've
trained my brain to take in the smallest of details of every
experience. The color. The smell. The degree of difficulty.
The people enjoying or not enjoying it with me. The vibe. The
freshness. The cliché. What would I do differently? Why is this
succeeding or failing?

I write my thoughts down. Or, I speak them into my phone.

Here's the greatest thing I can tell you right at the start: *Write your ideas down.* Ideas come and go. They will most certainly go if you don't trap them.

Ideas are highly marketable commodities.

Ideas will make *you* marketable.

Over the last three decades, my bio has blossomed. Artist. Speaker. Painter. Musician. Songwriter. Author. Blogger. Consultant. Conference leader. Experience Designer. Teacher. Pastor. Architect. Contractor. Poet. Storyteller. Interior Designer. Concert Promoter. Thankfully, I've always worked in environments where I could expand my bio while staying on task. I've been able to do the things I love and create experiences for people that line up with the job I'm being paid to do.

A wise man once told me when I was getting ready to get married, "Find something you love to do and then find a way to get paid for it." That's great proverbial advice (which we'll challenge a bit later), but many wouldn't remotely know how to even begin to achieve that ideal. Very few can stand up one day and say, "I quit! I'm going to find something I love and find a way to get paid for it." Unless the thing they love is begging for cash on a street corner.

What if, no matter what you are currently doing, you could find ways to sharpen your mind to become an Idea Mentalist? Then, what if you brought the ideas you would love to be a part of to your current job—creating a world where your ideas give you a new level of job security? What if those ideas then revolutionized your workplace? And, what if you started loving that job more than you ever dreamed possible?

Or, what if those ideas caught the attention of someone else and you were then sought after? And what if—because of your idea-ability—you know that if it all ended tomorrow, you had it within you to create something *ex nihilo* and forge a new path? Then, you could truly find something you love and find a way to get paid for it.

No matter what organization you work for, I will guarantee you the owner of your company does not want to become stagnant. They don't want to become a thing of the past. Your organization knows if it is starting to stagnate it is on the path to dying. The world is changing all around your organization.

This also means that if you don't have ideas, you may be exactly the opposite of marketable—*expendable*. I don't mean at the core of who you are. You are a beautiful human with potential to be the best possible version of yourself. But, when it comes to the workplace or making your own way as an entrepreneur, you need an idea bank.

I also have experience as an employer. My favorite people on my teams have always been idea people. The people who are bringing ideas to the table and seeing them through to fruition will always have a place on my teams. Nothing is more boring (or sometimes infuriating) than the person who is not motivated to do or be different for the sake of the vision.

Whether I've worked for someone or I've been the one hiring people to work for me, I've learned employers want ideas. Employers want *idea people.*

Employee.
Employer.
Stay-at-home parent.
Young.
Old.
Entrepreneur.

Business owner.
Teacher.
Contractor.
Recent graduate.
Risk-taker.
Artist.
Craftsperson.

You need ideas.

There's No Idea Incantation

A *mentalist* is a performance artist that seems to have super-human—or at least highly developed—mental abilities and/or keen insight. They're the performers that make you say, "What just happened?" The hypnotists. The fortune tellers. The mind readers. Some mentalists combine more traditional magic components to their act and are often known as mental magicians—two of the most famous being David Blaine and Criss Angel.

Like the performance mentalist, the Idea Mentalist wows the crowd. They make people say, "Where does she come up with this?" They have people scratching their heads, saying, "I wish I was that creative." And also, like the performance mentalist, the Idea Mentalist knows it takes a lot of work to get there. There really is no magic incantation that one says before a brainstorming meeting to make the office want to take charge on a new innovation.

I sold insurance as a young man. It looked like an easy way to make money from my youthful perspective. I told this one day to my manager who looked at me and laughed. "The sweat has to come from somewhere," he said. He was right. The month I quit, I had lost thirty pounds and was vomiting almost every day from stress. Not the kind of sweating that was healthy for me. Every job I've had since then proved him right.

You will have to sweat for your *ideas*.

I wish I had a dollar for every time someone asked me, "How come ideas come so easy to you?" I get it. I consider myself an Idea Mentalist. But I know a secret they don't always know. I've worked hard for my ideas. I've mined for them. I've toiled for them. And, they don't know all my ideas that didn't work. They don't know all the ideas people have told me are stupid. They don't know the ideas I eventually thought were stupid.

Ideas breed new ideas. You get new ideas from the death of the old ideas. You get new ideas in the middle of ideas. You get new ideas by paying attention to others' ideas and comatose ideas and ideas that bit the dust.

I have notebooks full of ideas. Ready for the right time. Or, in some cases, the wrong time. But I won't know that until I launch the idea. Then I'll learn. And the next idea is right around the corner.

Some of you reading this book are on the precipice of a risky venture. You are full of energy and expectation. You are about to launch forward with the greatest idea ever. You're full of certainty.

That's fantastic. I know the feeling. I've been there many times. And, one thing I know for sure is your idea—in its current state—has a shelf life.

You will get *bored*.
Or it will *stop working*.
Or the world will change and make it *obsolete*.

It's okay. It just means you need more ideas. You have to keep thinking and creating and trying. Ideas come from *hard work*.

Idea muscles need to be stretched and worked or they atrophy.

Ideas are found in running streams. Not stagnant pools.

Ideas aren't magic. The sweat has to come from somewhere.

To Become Intelligent, You Must Become Ignorant

Idea Mentalists understand the more we know, the more we don't know. Or, a better way to say it may be: the more we know, the more we become aware of what we've *yet to know*. And, the more we know, the more we're able to challenge ourselves and be challenged about the things we thought we knew and think we know. This makes us smarter. You know?

Teenagers (in my experience) are the "smartest" people in the world. We say things to them like, "You think you know it all." And they do. *As far as they know*. But, intelligence is more an acknowledgement of what you don't know than it is a proclamation of what you do know.

We will say things about the teenage mindset (and often with adults who assume the same posture) like, "They know just enough to be dangerous." But, that's not entirely true. What we really mean is, "They think they know enough," and that makes them dangerous. It's not that they're dumb. Not at all. My youngest daughter, as a teen, was one of the smartest people I've ever met. And, at the same time, she didn't possess the decades of experiences I have. Every once in a while, I would think, "Wow. She's really smart. But, what she doesn't know is _____."

Idea Mentalists don't underestimate the knowledge that comes with living out one's years—however many they are blessed with. They also don't underestimate the knowledge that comes with *experiences* through the years. Maturity plays a part, for sure, but one can also be younger-and-smarter because of their experiences or older-and-not-as-smart because of their lack of experiences. Some smarts come naturally with time and maturity, and some smarts come with *exposure* and *experience*.

I met a woman in her young twenties once as I was playing music in Europe. She had traveled through over fifty countries already. She tasted the various cuisines. She talked with the people. She walked the streets. She hiked the backcountry. She rode the trains, planes, boats, taxis, buses, subways, horses, motorcycles, rickshaws, and trolleys in various places. She learned multiple languages.

Is there any guarantee that she is going to come up with an idea that changes the world, or even her world? No guarantee. But, outside of being born with some super-human capacity to conjure up world-changing ideas, does her experience position her to think differently, process differently, rationalize differently, troubleshoot differently, conceptualize differently, and anticipate conflict differently than the average Joe who sits in an armchair all day watching the news? You betcha.

There is perhaps no easier arena to recognize this *exposure-and-experience-count* truth than on social media during a political debate (of any kind). As both sides loudly share their *surefire* ways to fix a problem, the shared ignorance can be deafening and frightening to those more intimately acquainted with the outlying issues and problems the *foolproof* idea-folks are painfully unaware of.

I once heard a scientist give an explanation of string theory. He blew my mind with his knowledge, metaphors, mathematics, and propositions. He did such a great job of taking top-shelf science and packaging it for a commoner and peasant in the world of science—like me. As my brain downloaded the information, I felt smarter (for about five minutes) as I thought to myself, "I get it. Makes sense. I can even explain a lot of this to someone else."

But then, he gave an incredibly long list of things he did *not* know about the way the universe works. He introduced terms I had never heard before. He spoke with authority about what he was ignorant of. As he spoke about what he didn't know, I became dumber about string theory, and he appeared even smarter to me. He knew something of what he had yet to know, but I didn't even know the questions he was asking existed.

I know nothing about string theory if I'm honest. Just because I thought about it for five minutes (and felt pretty smart) did not make me *know* it. The way I felt about myself in those five minutes (like a cocky teenager) also did not make me *know* it. Seeing the models and equations did not make me *know* it—I didn't even understand what I was looking at. I have not done the hard work of *knowing*. Knowing requires *experience*. I have not *experienced* the things I need to experience to *know* string theory.

Think of yourself as a sponge in a large body of water (intelligence). Everywhere the surface of the sponge touches the water are the boundaries of your ignorance. As the sponge soaks up (experiences) the water, it becomes fuller. However, at the same time, the surface of the sponge has also become larger. The sponge now knows that there's more to be known than when it first got introduced to the water. The sponge becomes more aware of what it doesn't know as it touches more of the water. To *know,* then, is to *experience* more. So, when it comes to new experiences, soak them in.

Why is this so important in the world of ideas? Because the more experiences we have, the more we are able to predict the future, the more we are able to understand various applications, the more we are able to guesstimate what works and what doesn't, the more we are able to anticipate the pushback of naysayers, the more we are able to see what the competition doesn't see, the more we are able to ask questions of the things that others aren't even aware are things to consider, and the more we are able to discern what we don't yet know and are still to know.

CHAPTER TWO
CREATION

Then There Was an Idea

For our purposes, an idea is a *new* thought introduced to the present situation as a proposal for a course of action.

That doesn't mean an idea can't resemble something you've never seen before (although those ideas exist, and we'll explore how to mine for them). But, by definition (in our context), an idea is something that hasn't been thought of for the particular situation or problem at hand. If it's not new, it's not helpful.

The ideas we're talking about in this book are *helpful*. To someone. To an organization. To yourself. To the world.

We label non-helpful and not-new suggestions as tired, old hat, unthoughtful, boring, regurgitated, dull, exhausted. Unfortunately, people all around us offer up non-helpful and not-new solutions all the time. And many times, others will act on those not-ideas because no one stands up and says, "Are you kidding me? That's the same thing we've always done." Or, "That sounds just like the thing the other guys did and it didn't work." Or, "Hey, we're better than that." No one says these things because they have no ideas. Or, they fear getting fired. Or, they're timid. But, most likely, it's the no-idea thing.

Or, maybe they have an idea, but they're not sure anyone is going to like it. Because, it's way different. Or, because they've never seen a prototype. Or, it's not fully formulated. Or, they haven't figured out the *how*. Or, they don't want to get teased. Or, they don't know if the resources will support it. Or . . .

Speak up!

And the Idea Was Good

There are many different kinds of ideas and they come from many different kinds of wiring. Sometimes your idea may not work at all, but it sparks another idea that wows everyone. And blows minds. And moves everyone forward. And creates energy. And revenue. And pride.

So, start.

Once you start sharing good ideas, it's easier to find and share more. Did you catch that? When you share an idea and people acknowledge it as *good*, you're more likely to unearth more ideas. It feels good to be rewarded for good ideas.

Start taking note of the things, places, situations, times of day, weather, surroundings, postures, and energy that breed ideas for you. Write those down as you go through this book. They are your friends.

Idea factories are built. Fashioned, formed, shaped, crafted, created. But, they start as work sheds. Factories are built by gurus who started at some point as eager and green entrepreneurs. They're built only after investing time and being saturated in the idea industry.

Idea Mentalists take out small idea loans before they build their own empire. Like songwriters, they spend years playing the dive bars and covering other songwriters' material. All the time, they are writing their own song(s). They try it on for size. Sometimes the audience hates it. They keep on keeping on. Till they get a hit.

Part of the songwriter's journey is to figure out who they are. What is *their* sound? That comes with time. And multiple tries. And hard experiences. And input. And helpful criticism.

Criticism. I've heard many times, "In every bit of criticism, no matter how hurtful, there is always some truth." That is a lie from the pit of hell. Not that there is *never* truth in criticism—there just certainly isn't *always* truth in criticism. If you go on thinking you should learn something from every negative thing someone says about you, you will end up depressed and self-loathing. And broken. And your ideas will start to dry up as your energy feeds the ugly lies.

Sometimes when people criticize your idea, it's because they're intimidated by you. Or, they don't like you. Or, they're mad at themselves for not having ideas. Or, they're threatened by you. Or, they've allowed fear or tradition to eclipse their good judgment. Or, they're jealous. Or, they've been hurt by something else and they're taking it out on you. Or, they're weak. Or, they're just horrible people.

Sometimes people will criticize your idea because it isn't the way *they* would do it. That doesn't make your idea bad. Sometimes they criticize your idea because it doesn't fit the organization's goals. That may be true. They may be right. But, it doesn't make your idea bad. Sometimes they criticize your idea because the timing isn't right. That may also be true. So, recognize that for what it is and hold on to your idea for another time or another version of the same idea.

You're a creative person. With ideas. They're in there. You're wired for ideas. You need to know what kind of wiring you have. And harness it. And utilize it. And sharpen it. And celebrate it.

There are all kinds of *idea people*. Let me suggest a few.

Some people are Artisans. Artisans make things. They take the stuff in their head, and they turn it into a thing. You can touch their ideas. See their ideas. Walk through their ideas. Experience their ideas. Hang their ideas on your wall. Use their ideas in the kitchen.

Artisans bring a special something to their ideas that only they can. In some mediums, technology seems to have leveled the playing field because it's so easy to create things with software that once were only possible by finding a skilled artisan. But, you know the magical artisan when you see their work. We can all work our way around Instagram and feel like a rockstar, but artisans bring a special something to their work that only they can. Even when technology makes it easier for the rest of us to create, the artisans rise above and use the technology to their advantage. They outshine those of us who aren't artisans in that medium.

Side note: Just because you're an artisan, it doesn't necessarily mean you are a multidisciplinary artisan. Though, you may be.

Some people are Originators. Originators make things up. Not that they don't steal and build upon—they can do that as well. But the originator—the creative idea inventor—will often produce the shocker. They will surface the bizarre. They will confuse people. They change our view of art and ideas. They create *ex nihilo*—out of nothing.

They ask, "What if those crazy ideas in my head are supposed to be acted upon? What if making that outrageous decision to do that thing people laugh at is one of the most important things I can do for my company, or school, or church, or community, or family, or business, or non-profit at this time?"

Some people are Assemblers. Assemblers are curators. Pulling in different elements and themes. They think in terms of series' and collections. Their ideas bring theories and technologies and colors and vibes and art and people and materials together.

These people do things like put on conferences that are unexpected and challenge the concept of what a conference is. They know how to pick just the right entertainment to match the keynote speaker who will rip our hearts out. They have us cutting a check at the end of the experience because we are moved to do something. We are changed because of their idea, which may be a collection of ideas culminating into another.

They are the kind of people that can pull a bunch of junk together and sell it for stupid amounts of money. They build theme parks. They launch festivals. They rejuvenate cities. They put together dream teams.

They are the people you want throwing your staff Christmas party and designing your new brochure and reinventing your office space.

Some people are Aestheticians. Aestheticians make things beautiful. Or they see beauty where there's none apparent to the average person. They see what can be. Their ideas redeem things.

These are the people who don't see a junkyard; they see a park. They don't see graffiti; they see a mentoring program for young artists. They don't see the homeless cluttering the streets; they see an opportunity to raise awareness and financial means to create new kinds of homeless shelters and rehabilitation programs. They don't see a music program being cut from a school; they see a teen center with live music capabilities, a place for young musicians to record demos, a coffee shop, homework tutors, and an environment that is infinitely better than band class.

They dream of phoenixes rising from the ashes. Their ideas rescue and revitalize. Their ideas may breathe new life without having to spend a bajillion dollars. They are the found-object artists.

Some people are Provocateurs. Provocateurs sense a disturbance in the Force and their ideas come from a conscientious response to that disturbance. Their ideas are designed to make the world a better place by poking the bear.

They often make people angry with their ideas and that's a good gauge for them.

They are the censored poets and writers, the artists that point out the ugly things, the march-against leaders, the protest songwriters, the status-quo questioners, and the system-fighters. They're not always loud, but their ideas scream.

My friend Rix is an artist. And an idea provocateur. On many occasions, I've seen grown humans talk with Rix about his art and be moved to tears. Sometimes, he can't really explain his own art in a way that is satisfying to linear thinkers. All they know is, they must own it. It stirs something within them. Rix is often angered by mediocrity, injustice, and people wonder if he sometimes provokes just to get attention. If he does, it's not for his own gain. Yes, he sometimes makes a spectacle of himself in the strangest ways and his creations draw attention. But, his ideas cause us to think differently and react differently.

Some people are Prophets. Prophets trade in the world of visions and dreams. They see things that no one else sees. They hear things no one else hears. Prophets are often disliked because it is common for them to think differently than what is commonly accepted and typical. Prophets pave new roads. Prophets are allergic to the status quo.

Prophets reorient us. They cause us to see things differently, in ways that rejuvenate us and remind us of the things we love. They capture us and rapture us. They make us feel young again.

Some people have a dose of all the above or at least a mixture of some.

You are unique. You have a certain you-ness that no one has. Your ideas will be different simply because you are you. Find out who you are. Embrace it. Celebrate it. Know the specific *you* that creates ideas.

CHAPTER THREE
PHILOSOPHY OF AN IDEA MENTALIST

Philosophy is the study of the theories of knowledge or experiences. It's about the nature of reality and existence. It's about belief systems. I know, all of that seems *so* esoteric. Let's make it easy.

A personal philosophy about anything describes:

Why you do
What you do
In the way you *do it.*

It's as simple as that.

You want to be able to answer questions like, "What makes you think that?" with statements like, "Because, I have a deep-seated belief that _____."

When someone says, "I don't think that's a good idea," you want to be able to ask them why.

When they don't have a good answer, you want to have one ready. You want to be confident about your ideas. To be confident about your ideas, you need to know why you believe in them. You want to know the deep-seated beliefs you have about people and systems and business and life and your organization.

This chapter is full of the tenets of an Idea Mentalist philosophy. Let them marinate.

TENET ONE
"Who Says We Can't Do That?"

It's the most important question an Idea Mentalist asks themselves. Learn to ask it. Make it yours.

Fear and tradition choke the life out of new ideas. Fear of failure, embarrassment, challenge, and what others might think are mortal enemies of the idea. But, even greater than this enemy is tradition—*the way we've always done it.*

Tradition can massacre ideas. Companies. Churches. Governments. Party platforms. Learning institutions. Family businesses. Families. Not that tradition is always bad. Some can be helpful in creating a sense of peace, expectation, camaraderie, stability, and good vibes. But when it goes bad, it goes very bad. When an organization is struggling because of its unwillingness to change, adapt, overcome, and risk, it gets one step closer to death with every slippery foothold.

Charles Kettering—inventor of the battery powered starter for the automobile—is credited with this quotation about change:

> "I am not pleading with you to make changes, I am telling you you have got to make them - not because I say so, but because old Father Time will take care of you if you don't change. Consequently, you need a procurement department for new ideas."

I imagine that procurement department having a sign on the wall that says, "***Who says we can't do that?***"

If you want to be an Idea Mentalist, you need to ask the question, "Who says we can't do that?" like a two-year old. Over and over. Or, your ideas will atrophy. You won't flourish.

When you ask the question, "Who says we can't do that?" you can begin to eliminate all barriers to making your idea a reality.

An energetic "Who says we can't do that?" is the rallying cry to gather the troops and charge.

And great things might just happen.

Let me tell you a couple of stories from my own life where this question has proven to be the best question I could have asked.

I lived for over a decade in the Midwest. The town that I lived in had its own local TV station. I fostered a relationship with these folks at the station and we partnered together on some fun projects. I was a guest on their show a few times as a local musician, promoter, and artist.

One day, the TV station called me and asked if I would come to the studio to help them work on a jingle. I had written some jingles in the past and I think I have a knack for catchy hooks and melodies. So, I obliged. Just as a favor. Things were really busy for me, but it wasn't going to take much time.

"Who says I can't do a favor?"
"Who says I'm not the man for the job?"
"Who says I don't have the time?"

When I got to the station, I was greeted by one of the production staff.

Him: "He's here."
Me: "Who's here?"
Him: "The COO."
Me: "The COO of what?"
Him: "Did nobody tell you what was happening today?"
Me: "Yeah, I got a call that you guys wanted some ideas for a jingle. But, I don't even know what for yet."
Him: "We'll catch you up to speed. Come on up."

And up the stairs we went. I was escorted to the war room of the studio and was introduced to the COO of a large company that worked with the airlines. I was asked to take a seat at the round table where five of us sat—the COO, the owner of the television station, two from production staff, and me.

The COO represented the company that was commissioning the station to make a video and create a jingle to promote safety in their operation. Even though the station was small, they had a great personal relationship with the COO that was developed because of their local sports coverage and the fact that the COO had a son or a nephew or knew someone on a local team. It was a big project, but they were up for the challenge.

"Who says a small-town studio can't do something big?"

The COO told me what they were looking for. Each year, they did a new creative safety-awareness project. This year, they were thinking about parodying a popular song and using that to talk about safety issues. "Like Weird Al," he said.

I appreciate Weird Al. But as a songwriter, I have developed an allergic reaction to many parodies. Mostly because I think they're lazy songwriting. And, oftentimes they're too kitschy for my liking. Sometimes, I think they're funny. I've written them. But I don't trust them. I'm not confident in them. Too many variables. These were the thoughts that raced through my mind as he talked.

They wanted the song to be an intro to their video. "What's the video like?" I asked. They told me the previous year they did a parody video of the guy from the Allstate ads, Mr. Mayhem. They thought about bringing Mr. Faux-Mayhem back this year too. It was the kind of thing people had come to *expect*.

All eyes were on me. And I don't have a poker face.

A song parody coupled with a video parody is not my cup of tea. And, I also know that just because people *expect* something, it doesn't make it good. So, I took a risk. Because I had absolutely nothing to lose.

"I think you're better than that," I said. "I also think we have enough talent around this table to create something original that will stick in people's heads the entire length of your campaign and beyond." They smiled. Nervously, I imagine.

Then, I asked the big question, *"Who says we can't do something different than what they expect?* You guys lead your companies!" They chuckled in what I think was amusement.

I asked the COO to tell me more about safety at his company and what I needed to know about it. He told me about all the things that could potentially go wrong if safety wasn't a priority. He told me how employees talk about being safe so everyone makes it home that night. He told me about a recent accident they had where someone lost his life as a result of a careless mistake.

As he was talking, I was reminded of something I saw painted on a wall at the Bonnaroo Music and Arts Festival one year. I told my friends around the table how I saw the words "Don't be THAT guy" tagged near the entrance of the festival grounds. The phrase was to remind concertgoers of the stupid people that do dumb things at concerts like drink a bunch of alcohol, forget to eat or drink water, and dance naked in the sun in the sweltering Tennessee heat. Nobody likes *that guy*. *That guy* vomits on his friends. *That guy* makes his friends miss a show because they have to take him to the First Aid tent. *That guy* yells "USA! USA! USA!" while pumping his fists and everyone is trying to listen to the show. Yeah, don't be *that guy*.

I began my pitch. I shared my Bonnaroo musings. "In your own organization, the people who ignore safety are *that guy*. What if we create a whole campaign around that idea of not being *that guy* complete with an original song and music video?"

"I love it," the COO said with great enthusiasm. "But it's not what we're used to. I don't know how it will fly with her."

"Who is *her*?" I asked.

Before anyone could answer the question, the COO was already dialing the *president and owner* of the company. And putting *her* on speaker phone. As it was ringing, he whispered something to me about how the idea might not fly with *her* because he didn't know if she'd like the change of direction.

Apparently, when I asked the question, *"Who says we can't do that?"* I wasn't taking into consideration that there may be someone the COO had to answer to. But the point here is, most of the time the "who" in the "who says" is referring to an imaginary audience. Or fear. Or tradition. There isn't always a literal "who" that is guarding the gates. There usually isn't a "who" that is going to get you in trouble. If the "who" in this case was the president and owner of the company, that was easy. If she didn't like it, we'd find a new idea.

The COO started out with, "The creative guy is here in the room with us and he's going to tell you all about the plan. It's amazing."

All eyes were on me. Again.

My "plan" was unfolding before my own ears as well as theirs. I threw a bunch of ideas out about scripting, and storyboarding, and staging, and location, and style.

Because, *"Who says I shouldn't be able to direct this?"*

When I stopped talking, the speakerphone in the middle of the table said:

"Hire him."

Everyone relaxed in their chairs a bit and started laughing. It was on!

The president is a really nice lady. I've enjoyed talking with her on a few different occasions over the years since our first virtual meeting. She isn't a big bad wolf huffing and puffing to blow an idea down. It's just that no one had asked her to do anything different up to that point. They expected the same kind of something (tradition), and no one had taken a risk to ask her to change it (fear).

When the COO left the room, I asked the owner of the station, "So, how does this work? I came here to consult and ended up getting hired by the president, but I think I actually work for you in this situation, right?" He told me candidly how much money they had contracted the whole thing for (not much and not enough) and asked me if I could draw up a contract between me and the station to pay me for my idea and time. We worked out a fair deal for both of us with the small amount we had to work with.

That one idea and that one question sparked a series of events that would become my biggest side-hustle of the following year. One idea and one question lead to other ideas that would find me writing a song and starring as the main character in the music video filmed on location at Detroit's DTW airport. I forged multiple separate contracts for my time and ideas.

"What if we filmed it at the airport during business hours?" No one had ever done it post-9/11, but, *"Who says we can't do it?"*

"What if we got some employees to star in it with me? It would give them more buy-in to the concept and the campaign." No one had ever asked that before but, *"Who says we can't do it?"*

"Can I curl my mustache and wear a top hat for the film so I look more character-like?" Well, there's no real video dress code so, *"Who says we can't do that?!"*

I was also hired to interview people at their annual safety fair for a documentary. I was honored to be invited to be the keynote speaker at their annual event in Chicago where leaders from all over the country gathered to talk about safety. At that event, they gave away merchandise with my likeness and top hats—like I wore in the music video—emblazoned with, "Don't be that guy!" I was contracted to sing with a band at the after party. The following year, I was contracted to write an original song for their anniversary celebration.

I tell you this story about myself not to brag. I tell you the story to celebrate it with you. Because, I know the power of the question, *"Who says we can't do that?"* I've made a habit out of it, and I know it can help you. I want you to know I'm not just talking about a theory or a hex the question puts on someone. It's not a manipulative question or a get-rich-quick scheme.

When no one asks the question, nothing changes. Many of you need to experience drastic change. Change that will take time. But, you need to start with this question.

"Who says we can't do that?" is the first critical question and tenet of a good philosophy of ideas. Now, let's look at a few more essential ingredients to the Idea Mentalist philosophy.

TENET TWO
Break Your Own Rules

Surprise! "Who says we can't do that?" also applies to you. In order to become an Idea Mentalist, you need to think differently than you've thought before. As a matter of fact, from now on, think of yourself as not having a *way of thinking*.

Many humans are more set in their ways than they care to admit. Habits. Routines. Preferences. Likes. Tastes. All good things unless they stifle one's ability to invent ideas. It is perfectly fine to have a special thing you are known for. But after a while, your special thing runs the risk of not being special anymore.

My wife used to watch a certain TV show that shall go unnamed. I'm not a huge fan. I fear if I name it, I will somehow be murdered by countless forty-to-fifty-something year old women who worship at the altar of HGTV. One evening, while watching this show, I asked my wife, "Why is everything white and gray? All the time?" I like their design ideas for the most part, but it's all the same color palette. Now, some might argue with me and point out they use many different colors on this show. True. Alabaster. Silver Strand. Oyster Bay. Repose Gray. Mindful Gray. Five different colors. Those are the most popular. All white and gray. Ish.

At first, it was good. There wasn't another show that had this same flair. Then, everybody started painting everything white. And gray. But, mostly white. Whitewashing as well. Many stores popped up in my town (and many other towns) full of white furniture. I mean, all white. Repurposed, white furniture. And people ate it up.

For about a year. Then, many stores that counted on the white and gray craze went out of business. For two reasons. One: People figured out they could just paint their existing stuff white on their own. Two: All white stuff is boring after a while. The TV show got boring too.

There is an unfortunate fallout of television shows like this (although I don't want to completely demonize them). I will guarantee you that there are homes FILLED with all-white furniture right now as a result of this show and this trend AND they will stay like that for a long, long time. Because, no one is going to walk into your home and say it's boring. No one is going to say, "You know, all-white went out of style already." But, after a few years, they are certainly going to think it. The only person that is going to change the color one day is you.

When you ask yourself, "Who says I can't do that?"

I'm painting with large brush strokes (pun intended. Couldn't resist.) here. If you like the unmentioned show and your house is all white, I am sorry if I offended you. You can enjoy your white stuff as long as you want. It's yours. You can turn it right around on me and say, "Who says I can't keep my whitewashed birdcage against my alabaster shiplap wall?" And, I hope you do. If you feel that way. I actually like the birdcage and the wall.

But, one day you are going to have to choose. Please don't let fear or tradition keep you from choosing. One day, the shiplap is going to hit the fan and you are going to have to innovate.

The job you've had forever might be killing you. You need a new idea for making a living. *Who says you can't do that?* Maybe the job you want is in the same company, but you need to prove you are the person for it. You need an idea. Then, you will grab their attention. *Who says you can't do that?* Maybe your job is killing you because it isn't working but you have an idea to make it go easier for everyone. *Who says you can't bring that up?* Maybe, your idea is to start a new chapter in a different city and start a business where you sell all black furniture. *Who says you can't do that?*

Obviously, this is more than a story. It's a metaphor.

Which brings us to our new philosophical gem.

TENET THREE
Everything is a Metaphor for Something

Have you ever been watching a movie about a football team who had something tragic happen and yet the team goes all the way to the top to beat the odds and take home the trophy and you say to yourself, "Wait a minute! This isn't a movie about football at all. Isn't it about human struggle?" Or, have you been reading a story in a book about a girl who is told she's ugly all her life and then finds out she's a princess and all of a sudden people love her and you think to yourself, "Wait a minute! Isn't this actually about significance and identity and the struggle to be known?" And, when you read those stories and watch those movies, do you ever think, "This is kinda about me?"

That's because everything is a metaphor. Metaphors teach us about life and ourselves and our situations. We recognize metaphors in narratives because they are the same thing. Metaphors are just condensed, simplified, streamlined narrative. Easy to swallow in little bites. Narratives or stories are just metaphors on a large scale—adorned and decorated with details and plot twists and soundtracks and character development. Narratives and metaphors feed ideas.

I dare you to read a biography about Steve Jobs and not be inspired. When you read stories about how Steve came in at the last minute and trashed a project they had spent thousands of hours on because the design wasn't sexy enough, ask yourself, "Who am I in the story? Jobs? Or, am I the guy slaving away on something without thinking about the main goal, which is obviously to make it sexy?"

And, when you read these stories, watch these movies, and digest these biographies, ask yourself, "What is my goal? Am I reaching it? Am I helping the company's goal? What is that? What is my not-sexy-enough thing that should be trashed?"

Allow stories, and situations, and entertainment, and walks through the park, and exercise, and coffee dates, and lunch appointments, and trips to Lowes or Home Depot be a metaphor. Because, they are. For something. Metaphors are all around.

One of the ways you can pay attention to the metaphors all around you is to get the backstories. Behind every situation, story, decision, idea, is a backstory. The company you work for has a backstory. Someone started it. For a reason. They had original staff members. Some were fired. Some left legacies. Some invested and bled for the company.

Imagine this: One day, you're charged with remodeling the office. You have brilliant ideas full of colors and textures and arrangements. But, a few people don't have the same excitement as you. You get frustrated. Even angry. You can't understand why people don't like your ideas. They're frickin' amazing. You'll make more space, bring more light, make it more hip. Give it that *joie de vivre* feeling that's missing.

What you don't know is that five years ago, Steve was asked to remodel. He didn't do anything. He talked a lot about it but did nothing. When someone opposed Steve's ideas, Steve lashed out by telling stories about them behind their back. Steve was eventually fired.

You don't know Steve. But, what everyone else knows is remodeling the office is a metaphor for frustration and hurt feelings. Good to know.

Furthermore, your idea to get rid of that "big old clunky desk" up front ruffled feathers because the desk was made by Nick. Nick was the nicest guy you could ever meet. He always complimented people on their work. He would give you the shirt off his back. He helped your boss get through her divorce by being a listening ear. And, he tutored kids in an after-school program because he used to be a teacher and absolutely loved kids. You didn't meet him though, because he's dead.

The desk is a metaphor for hard work and craftsmanship and loyalty and love and beautiful things and the kind of change that makes people sad. You didn't know Nick. Or about the desk.

So, how could your ideas help this situation if you knew the backstory?

Well, first you could have a meeting with the employees. You could ask them about their hopes and dreams for the office and what kind of an environment they dream of working in. You could ask them if they've ever been through a remodeling project before. You could ask them about the desk.

Once you heard all the stories about Steve and Nick and everyone else, you could have presented your ideas differently in a way that celebrates the office and its past. Then you could help them create new metaphors for the changes about to come.

Maybe Nick's desk gets repurposed as a beautiful central table. Maybe the desk gets milled into smaller pieces and you build a plaque out of the wood for the wall with Nick's photo on it. Maybe the desk is sold, and the money donated to a scholarship fund for kids of office staff. Maybe Nick's desk becomes the welcome table in the newly remodeled lobby.

In any number of situations, Nick's desk can now stand as a metaphor for legacy, hard work, good memories, the future, and hope. Maybe the way everyone was invited into the story and invited to be heard erases all memories of Steve the Jerk and remodeling now becomes a metaphor for teamwork and contribution and celebration.

Which leads us to our next good philosophy ah-ha . . .

TENET FOUR
There's Always an OPTION C

This one seems so easy, but it's often overlooked. How many times have you been in a discussion—with your spouse, boss, child, friend, or co-worker—and you come to an impasse when you can't decide between two ideas? It happens every day with the most trivial of decisions. We've grown accustomed to whittling down our choices to the two we're most comfortable with and/or the ones that have become the most routine for us.

*"**Mexican** or **Italian**?"*
*"Are you going to the gym **before** or **after** work?"*
*"**Romantic Comedy** or **Drama**?"*

We do the same with bigger decisions as well.

*"Should we send them to **private** school or **public** school?"*
*"Should we **fly** home for Christmas or **drive**?"*
*"Should we **keep trying** for this marriage or **call it quits**?"*

And, the workplace often presents A or B options for us.

*"Should we keep the office **open** on New Year's Day or should we **close** it?"*
*"Should we bid the job on a **time-plus-materials basis** or **quote it outright**?"*
*"Should we hire for this role as a **full-time** position or a **part-time** position?"*

It seems we've been conditioned to boil things down to two options. But, there is always an OPTION C. Idea Mentalists are always in search of the OPTION C.

OPTION C usually requires a lot more work.
OPTION C often calls out the fear.
OPTION C often kills a tradition.
OPTION C opens up a whole new world of opportunity and experience.
OPTION C is often the thing no one has ever tried before.

OPTION C is often scary.

OPTION C has the most variables.

OPTION C is the road less traveled.

OPTION C grabs people's attention.

OPTION C creates new memories.

OPTION C gets you recognized.

OPTION C is the unknown.

OPTION C is the *crème brûlée* to the status quo of the *"vanilla or chocolate ice cream?"* dilemma.

This is OPTION C in action:

*"**Mexican** or **Italian**?"*
OPTION C: Well, I had an idea this afternoon and decided to take you out for a picnic dinner. It's already in the car and ready to go. We're going to sit by the river and watch the boat show—which I know is one of your favorite things.

*"Are you going to the gym **before** or **after** work?"*
OPTION C: I decided to go to the gym on my lunch break. There are way fewer people there at that time.

*"**Romantic Comedy** or **Drama?**"*
OPTION C: How about we sit on the couch tonight and I read you a book?

*"Should we send them to **private** school or **public** school?"*
OPTION C: What would you think about the idea of homeschooling or unschooling them?

*"Should we **fly** home for Christmas or **drive**?"*
OPTION C: I was thinking we should check in to Amtrack. They have a sleeper car. It will take longer, but we can get work done on the train and see the country all the way from here to Seattle.

*"Should we **keep trying** for this marriage or **call it quits?**"*

OPTION C: I propose a separation. For a time. We could commit to going to counseling when we're apart from one another and go on a date once a week. Then, we can reevaluate in 6 months apart from all the drama we have in the house right now.

*"Should we keep the office **open** on New Year's Day or should we **close** it?"*
OPTION C: What would you think about keeping the front doors closed to the public but allowing employees to come in so they could work in a quiet environment?

*"Should we bid the job on a **time-plus-materials basis** or **quote it outright?"***
OPTION C: Why don't we bid it for time-plus-materials but give them a generous cap that we won't exceed?

*"Should we hire for this role as a **full-time** position or a **part-time** position?"*
OPTION C: Would you be willing to hire three people part-time? I think the job is too diverse for one person to handle it all. And, we'll save money since we won't have to pay benefits.

Often when OPTION C is presented, there is pushback. Mostly, the pushback comes because there is no precedent. People have a hard time dealing with OPTION C because they don't see how it will work.

Let's be honest. *You* might even be the person who struggles with OPTION C because *you* want to know how it will work. "How in the world . . . ?"

But, you want to be an Idea Mentalist. So get ready to embrace a new thought as part of your philosophy . . .

TENET FIVE
"How?" is the Wrong Question

Idea Mentalists often adopt a ready-fire-aim approach to ideas as part of their philosophy. They are okay not having all the answers at the beginning. They imagine the end result and don't get tripped up and stalled by the miniscule.

Idea Mentalists know that most of the how-questions that stop an idea from moving forward are easy to figure out *on the way* to seeing the idea to fruition. They are not intimidated by the unknown and the things they have yet to figure out. They know that once an idea is in motion, the original *questions-of-how* that seemed insurmountable to some are often tiny speedbumps—if they're bumps at all.

Once again, fear and tradition are the things that trip an idea up in the introduction phase. Here are a few phrases below to help you identify fear and tradition. They're all just another version of "How?" They all have OPTION Cs people are ignoring. Some are passive-aggressive ways of asking, "How?" Some are cocky. Many are full of speculation and second-guessing.

"What if the city doesn't approve it?"
"That sounds dangerous."
"Don't you think that's a bit expensive?"
"We don't have a budget for that."
"I don't think our people are ready for that."
"That's too controversial."
"I don't know that we can pull it off."
"I don't think we have the manpower."
"Sounds like that will take some time."
"Well, that'll never fly with the boss."
"That sounds great. How about a raise while you're asking?"
"And when do you plan on doing the job we hired you for?"
"I can already hear the complaints."

I've heard all these statements at one time or another in meetings over the years. Many times, these incognito how-questions stopped a new innovation right in its tracks. The Idea Mentalist needs to interrupt the how-questions with what I like to call *Prophetic Reorientation.*

Prophetic Reorientation is the art of visionary direction and redirection. When everyone else wants to surface the "How?" the Idea Mentalist calls for everyone to listen for the things no one hears and see the things not readily seen by others. They are masters of selling the sizzle, not the steak. They are aware of the present and tell the truth about it, but they constantly talk about the future and where we must head.

In order to silence the how-questions, they think way ahead of them. They are crafty with painting mind pictures of how it will be when the idea is a reality. They aren't abrasive and defensive (thought they will be tempted to be) when the how-questions arise. They confidently lean in to the questions and create a wow-factor. They do their homework and anticipate the "How?"

"What if the city doesn't approve it?"
I knew we'd like the idea, so I scheduled a meeting with them next week. I've already been casting vision.

"That sounds dangerous."
Obviously, we'd have to make sure it isn't. The building engineers can find the solutions. I plan on making one of them a team member to ensure safety.

"Don't you think that's a bit expensive?"
Yes. But not insurmountable.

"We don't have a budget for that."
No. We don't. But, imagine if money were not an object. Would we do it? I think so. That's why I'm talking to three investors

right now, putting together a sponsor package, and harnessing our creative team's ideas on financing. Plus, we have some back-end ideas on how this can bring in money.

"I don't think our people are ready for that."
They might not be. Let's get them ready. What are your ideas on how we can do that?

"That's too controversial."
Unless we get in front of it. I think we can pull a team together to help us vet potential controversy and come up with some healthy statements to cast vision on the front end and silence the controversy before it starts.

"I don't know that we can pull it off."
If we don't, someone else will. I think we're better than them.

"I don't think we have the manpower."
Probably not. I've already called the city to see if they have any interns they may want us to invest in that can help us along. Win-win.

"Sounds like that will take some time."
It will. But, with us all on board there is nothing that can stop us. I believe in this team.

"Well, that'll never fly with the boss."
Let's see if she's available. I'd love to hear her concerns so I can provide some clarity.

"That sounds great. How about a raise while you're asking?"
You're funny. I'll take a raise if you're willing to give it and I believe this idea may help you make that decision.

"And when do you plan on doing the job we hired you for?"
I plan to work just as hard as I always do. Also, I'm already starting on recruiting some volunteers to help make this a

reality. They are equally as excited to make this a reality. If at any point you see my work slacking, please come tell me.

"I can already hear the complaints."
I'd like to make a list of the people we think might have a complaint so I can take them out to coffee and cast some vision. I think they can be our best allies and cheerleaders once they understand.

Idea Mentalists never propose an idea without an accompanying story. Each idea that's brought to the table must have its own narrative that helps everyone experience the idea as if it already existed. A good portion of the time, the well-developed story will Jedi Mind Trick the how-questions into non-existence.

TENET SIX
It's Easier to Lower the Bar Than to Raise It

I'll never forget the first time I heard the phrase, "Reach for the stars but be content with the sky." I had a substitute Speech Communication professor once in college that owned stock in pithy grabbers. This guy opened his mouth and it sounded like a multi-volume set of *Chicken Soup for the Soul*. Bumper-sticker and t-shirt wisdom all day long. And, he used *this* syrupy phrase to encourage a student to use more vivid language in his speech.

As silly as it was to me then (and now), I've never forgotten that kitschy phrase. In many ways, it informs the way I think about ideas today. But, when we think about being "content with the sky," it doesn't mean "be fine with mediocrity." It just means that our original ideas are sometimes larger than can humanly be pulled off within a timeframe or budget and we need to be content—or gratified—by an equally excellent but smaller-scale likeness of that idea.

I can't stress enough how important this high-bar-setting thing is. Each idea and accompanying narrative must be full of vivid detail. Go big or go home. Larger than life. Go ahead, bite off more than you can chew. But give yourself permission to scale back.

It's way easier to produce an equally excellent and satisfying alter-version of your original idea than it is to be in the middle of the idea and convince everyone there needs to be more. Bigger? Better? More money? More time? More manpower? Those are fighting words when everyone is exhausted and elbows-deep in a project they just want to finish.

TENET SEVEN
Work Towards Version Four

No matter how good your idea is, always approach an idea with the expectation that you'll work and rework it to the best possible version it can be. This doesn't mean that you'll never have an idea that is not near-perfect out of the gate—you probably will have many of those. But, set yourself up for success. Don't get frustrated by the idea that is rough around the edges on the first or second pass. In the same way, don't relax after Version One of your idea.

Think of Version One as a prototype.

Invite critique from people you trust. Ask them to give you concrete feedback on your prototype. I always like to tell people, "You won't hurt my feelings at this point. This is the feedforward part." *Feedforward* is the good kind of criticism that helps you work out potential bugs before you launch.

Kim works as a Communication Director at her company. The company bought space—a booth—at a Christmas Tree Lighting ceremony so they could make the public aware of their business. They knew two things for sure: they wanted their booth to look inviting and they wanted to get people to hang around rather than pass by.

Version One: Kim pulled a team together. She worked with a designer on a logo that rhymed with the company's logo and celebrated the event. Someone else on the team lined up live music. Someone else made sure the booth was staffed. But, when all those details came together, the only thing that made it feel special was the live music (no one else was doing live music at the event). The team was asked to plan and come back together the following week, each with at least one new idea to propose.

Version Two: It was decided that music was fantastic, but people pass up musicians all the time. The team needed more of a hook—something to pull people in. Someone suggested giving away pieces of candy. Someone else suggested full-size candy bars would blow minds and be a worthy investment. Other booths would be giving away bite-sized treats and the team wanted to up the ante. "What if we wrap the candy bars in a new wrapper with our logo on it?" someone suggested. Kim got busy making the wrapper. As she worked away, she thought, "I should design this wrapper like a regular candy bar wrapper and make the ingredients list on the back mention a bunch of fun things about our company."

Version Three: The team loved what Kim did. It could have stopped right there. But, someone mentioned it was going to be cold outside where the booth was, and maybe the entire team should wear matching hoodies with the logo on them and offer a free hoodie to anyone who would volunteer that evening. Then, someone suggested another hook might be to place Golden Tickets (à la Willie Wonka) in a handful of the candy bars. The Golden Tickets could be an extra prize to make people feel special and perhaps make a friend who would then be interested in what the company had to offer. It was decided that the Golden Tickets would be gift cards for dinner for two at a local wine bistro. This would also be a great *support-the-local-businesses* move and the company would gain favor with the wine bistro.

Version Four: It could have stopped there. But, the team was committed to *Version Four*. So far, the booth would be decorated and filled beautifully with a snazzy logo on multiple surfaces and signs, live music, a smiling staff, and free candy bars that also advertised the company in a fun way and boasted the potential of a night on the town at a local business. But, when a team member suggested the Golden Ticket winners should come to the company office to retrieve their prize, the idea was leveraged to another level—getting people in the doors of the company was brilliant. This gave the company the opportunity to give tours to potential clients, have deeper conversation with the winners, and make a lasting impression. The team then decided to make the gift cards to the bistro only *part* of the prize and packaged the gift with swag from the company. To top it all off, one of the team members lined up a deal for a company rep to play live music at a local restaurant within walking distance of the Christmas booth. When people visited the restaurant, they would see the musician was sponsored by the company and perhaps visit the booth. If they showed up at the booth first, they would learn about the live music at the local restaurant and perhaps stay out later enjoying an evening that had been branded in two places.

Most people would stop with some variety of Version One. And, fair enough, live music was never part of this event. They were already going above and beyond. There would have been talk about their company following the event—how nice the staff was. How fun the music was. Version One was already enough to get by.

And if "enough to get by" is what you're looking for . . . settle with Version One. If *uniquely better, above the rest, get people talking, make a splash, sharpen your skills, go for broke, over the top,* and *be recognized for your work* is what you're after . . . work towards Version Four.

At the beginning of this chapter, we recognized that *fear* and *tradition* murder good ideas. I've mentioned it a few times since. It won't be the last time we talk about it.

Let's imagine some of the ways fear and tradition could have stopped Kim and her team. Some of the questions below are actual questions that came up during the team meetings.

"What if a kid grabs a chocolate bar without asking mom and he is allergic to chocolate? What if he gets sick? Will she come back and blame the company?"

"What if we run out of candy bars and people get angry because they didn't get one?"

"This event has never had live music. They probably won't want it there. It will probably bother the other booths and set a precedent they won't want to set."

"There probably isn't enough room in the booth to do all that."

"Won't this put us over budget? Where will the money come from?"

Fear and tradition. But, for the individuals and the teams who ask, *"Who says we can't do that?"* these questions are certainly not insurmountable, and some are laughable.

"What if a kid grabs a chocolate bar without asking mom and he is allergic to chocolate? What if he gets sick? Will she come back and blame the company?"
The kid *might* grab the chocolate. Kids do it all the time. Get over it.

"What if we run out of candy bars and people get angry because they didn't get one?"
If someone really gets angry because they didn't get a candy bar, get their address and tell them the company will send them one in the mail. Send them a whole box if that happens. Win them over.

"This event has never had live music. They probably won't want it there. It will probably bother the other booths and set a precedent they won't want to set."
The event has never had live music. It *might* be a problem. So, ask. They might deny your request. Or, you might be a trendsetter.

"There probably isn't enough room in the booth to do all that."
The booth might *not* be big enough. Set up a mock booth with the same dimensions and lay it all out before the event to make sure you can do it.

"Won't this put us over budget? Where will the money come from?"
It *will* go over budget. Talk to the person in charge of the budget and see where you might find some more money. Entertainment budget? Advertising budget? Holiday budget? If the answer is, "absolutely not," see if a store will donate the candy and be a co-sponsor. See if the bistro will donate some free dinners and be a co-sponsor.

So, how did Version Four go? The event was a big success. No kids got sick from chocolate. Many great conversations were had. The company spread good cheer. The live music at the booth was a success and kept folks hanging around. The live music at the local restaurant drew a huge crowd and the restaurant said it was their "biggest night" since they opened. The restaurant musician lined up multiple other gigs as a result of the exposure. The hoodies looked so good that others in the company wanted some and the company decided to buy more for the employees to wear around and advertise.

Two months later, everyone on the team realized that no one claimed the Golden Ticket prizes. Did that make it a failure? Absolutely not. The vibe and energy they created were worth the price of admission. Kim and her team decided to use the gift cards to celebrate the team's efforts and took them all to the bistro.

TENET EIGHT
Understand Incubating and Graduating

A commitment to the work of an Idea Mentalist acknowledges there are different stages to the idea process. When working with a team, Idea Mentalists model for everyone *how ideas grow*. Think of growing ideas in two stages: *incubation* and *graduation.*

Incubating

If you're a medical doctor, you might think of incubation in terms of a developing infection. The incubation period—in medical terms—begins when a pathogen enters the body and ends when the symptoms of the infection appear.

When it comes to ideas, that's a beautiful metaphor. Think of your ideas as being an infection—something that takes hold of you and begins to create change as it is fed. Soon, that infection has the potential to be passed on to others. It might even become epidemic or pandemic (words we are all too familiar with).

Or, you might think of incubation as an environment and diet that helps sustain and strengthen an infant in a premature state—another perfect use of the metaphor in relation to ideas.

The HBO show *Silicon Valley* is a story that follows a group of awkward techies that all live together in an incubator. In this case, the house they live in provides rent and utilities for free in exchange for monetary interest in the companies and products developed within. The incubator (house) removes distractions that might otherwise inhibit creative genius and allows ideas to flourish. This metaphor is also helpful for us as we think about becoming an Idea Mentalist.

For ideas to *incubate* well, set yourself up for success with the following:

- a commitment to *Version Four*
- an individual or team commitment to being *distinctively different*
- a belief that *no idea is impossible*
- an *inspiring space* to meet in

A commitment to Version Four means you absolutely need to communicate to your team that you're working towards it. Never settling on Version One. Tell the team you will be getting together a few times before the idea is solid (though, you should never think of your ideas as being so solid they can't be adapted). That way, no one will be frustrated in the process. Invite them to be excited with you as you watch the idea grow.

An individual or team commitment to being distinctively different means you and/or your team are committed to something special. Different. Not recycled. Innovative. New. Fresh.

You must understand that ideas, organizations, products, and the people behind them are easily forgotten and ignored when they become *predictable and routine*. Most people and organizations adopt the "if it's not broken don't fix it" rule even if they don't officially communicate those words. The French phrase *laissez-faire* means a policy or attitude of letting things take their own course, without interfering. Without adapting. Without changing. Without improving. Without asking, "Does this still work?" Idea Mentalists cannot be *laissez-faire*. Ever.

You must be aware that somewhere out there, someone is tweaking ideas and inventing new ways of doing things that will change the world. Some of those ideas will improve your situation. Some of those ideas have the power to kill your business. Or bury your idea. Or leave you in the dust.

Idea Mentalists are always asking how they can improve, change, twist, tweak, upgrade, refresh, undo, redo, renovate, and innovate. At some point, someone will copy your idea and do some improving, changing, twisting, tweaking, upgrading, refreshing, undoing, redoing, renovating, and innovating of their own. Then, your idea will no longer be distinctively different. That's the way it goes. The Idea Mentalist knows this and stays one to three steps ahead as often as possible.

A belief that no idea is impossible is more than being optimistic. It's more than believing humans have the ability to create things they dream of. It's a belief that all the stupid darts that get thrown from the naysayers—before your idea is even launched—must necessarily bounce off your thick skin. It's a belief that the demons in your head whispering that you are not good enough have never been helpful to anyone. It's a belief that conventional wisdom never blew minds.

This is personal.

An inspiring space to meet in means you may have to rethink where you dream, brainstorm, gather, hold meetings, write, invent, and create.

Many years ago, my friend asked me why I referred to my workspace as my "office."

I was confused. "Doesn't everyone call their workspace an office?"

He said, "Not artists. Doctors, for sure. But there has to be another name for the space for an artist."

I was blown away. By referring to my space as an office, I was creating a self-fulfilling prophecy. It was set up . . . like an office. It looked like . . . an office. It smelled like . . . an office.

I had created a space based on convention and what I thought others expected of my space. And, I lived that way for some time.

And, it was choking me.

I didn't realize just how much it had me by the jugular until I decided to change it.

After all, *"Who says you have to call it an office and design it like one?"*

If I'm honest, my first office space wasn't a "design" at all. It was functional but had no form. It was the lowest common denominator of office space with a few little things scattered here and there to give it some of my personality.

If I'm super-de-duper honest, even those little things that were scattered were not my personality at all. They were the personality I thought I was supposed to have. My office looked like some weird love child of Target, TJ Maxx, and Pottery Barn. Not that those stores are bad. They just aren't the places I would naturally gravitate towards if I gave a damn about design.

Which brought up the question for me, *"Why do I give a damn about design everywhere else and not my workspace?"*

My answers were telling, convicting, and sad. It was partly because I worried about what others thought about me, partly because of my guilty American work ethic coupled with some stupid unfounded fear of what a "fun" workspace might communicate to onlookers, and partly because I hadn't yet asked the question, *"Who says I can't do that?"*

I had allowed an *imaginary someone else* to effectively design my workspace for me. Marketers were selling me ideas all day long and I effectively gave them permission to make my workspace decisions for me. Tradition, fear, and convention had me by the balls. They stole my imagination. They stole my brand and recreated it in their image. They owned me and my wallet. All with my permission.

Almost overnight I changed the way my workspace was organized and arranged. I changed the overall aesthetic. It became a space that was inspiring to me.

Since that original makeover, my workspace has had many personality shifts. Because there are no rules. Because the office police are not watching. Because I have permission.

I want so badly for all of you to experience this kind of creative space freedom.

I renamed my workspace my *atelier* (French /adl'-yā). An atelier is a space where designers, artists, and artisans do their craft. Oftentimes with other artists. It's a place of imagination and creativity. Since then, I've had multiple ateliers in my life.

When I started writing this book, my atelier had a tin ceiling, striped walls with two different sheens of the same black paint that made it look like two colors, a repeated damask pattern stenciled on the walls that I designed, an oversized two-sided desk I picked up for sixty bucks that looks like it came out of Disney's Haunted Mansion, a 1901 pump organ made in Detroit, candelabras, a gargoyle on top of my bookcase, my collection of tobacco pipes, about seven guitars, a fireplace, original art from some of my friends, a turntable, and my entire collection of about 800 vinyl records. I sat in a tucked leather chair that was positioned across from a guest chair that looked straight out of Hogwarts.

Even as I enjoyed that atelier, I knew I would one day change it. Because there are no rules. Because the office police are not watching. Because I have permission. *PS, I had no idea when I wrote about the atelier above that my space would indeed change—because of outside forces. More on that later.*

Outside that atelier, in the corporate space at the "offices," is a space I named *The Playroom.*

The Playroom is a space where about twelve people can sit comfortably around a large wooden, gloss black table in the center of the room. The floor is made of varying colors and shades of wood laminate in a repeating pattern of white-wash, mahogany, ebony, and walnut. The outer wall has a large bay window that has been filled with a copper pipe contraption that is filled by multiple varieties of plants—making the window a sort of living wall. One entire wall, floor-to-ceiling, is a white dry-erasable surface. One wall is floor-to-ceiling with 50% chalk paint surface and 50% black dry-erasable surface for use with fluorescent pens. One wall has a giant television with a cork surface for pinning blueprints, drawings, news, photos, or any number of pin-worthy items. On the window wall, there is also a mounted roll of butcher paper. The door to the space is a rolling custom-made barn door.

No one ever accused my atelier or *The Playroom* of being stale. In these two spaces, great ideas were spawned. People wanted to hang out there. I'm convinced the time it took to go from *start* to *fidgety* for any meeting was drastically reduced in these spaces. The boredom-factor of a meeting is directly affected by the space in which that meeting is held. The engagement or lack thereof by participants in any meeting setting is directly proportional to the environment's perceived invitation and permission for interaction and participation.

A quick Google search will give you endless possibilities for creating your space, the science behind everything we've talked about, and hopefully a nagging sense that it is time to change your physical world and you have the permission or power to do so.

If you work with a team of people and you expect them to be creative, you need to either find or create space to meet that is inspiring. Whatever brand of inspiring works for you and your team.

Just imagine working in a space that inspires you and others to be the best possible version of yourselves. Imagine people coming to your space just because they've heard a buzz about it. If you already have that kind of space, I applaud you. You are in the minority. If you don't yet, I am so excited for you and what lies ahead.

One more thing designed to give you hope and inspiration: Because of the creative spaces I have designed and redesigned for myself over the years, I've been offered and accepted many space-design jobs over the years. I've designed restaurants, breweries, homes, lobbies, and office spaces as part of my side-hustle on many occasions. *Sometimes inadvertently, and quite by accident, the ideas you work out for yourself end up attracting the attention of others in ways you never dreamed.*

Graduating

Ideas must constantly graduate. Graduation means they must grow. They must begin to take on a life of their own. Ideas that don't graduate will die or at least lie dormant until they are revived. Think of graduation as forward momentum, putting feet to your dreams, actuation.

Graduation means you have to pull the trigger on your ideas. Sometimes, when they are half-baked. As you start to get your hands dirty with an idea, you'll understand better what you have to do in the next phase of incubation.

As ideas graduate, they reach new levels of incubation.

In the scholastic world, the first notable graduation is from high school. But, graduation does not mean you are necessarily finished with your schooling. You may go to junior college (a new incubation period). You may go to a four-year college after that (more incubation). Graduate and post-graduate work continue the incubation-graduation process.

It's the same with ideas.

Ideas don't just happen.

They are worked.
And reworked.
They are bred.
They are fed.
They are nurtured.

CHAPTER FOUR
PHILOSOPHY OF AN IDEA MENTALIST: PART DEUX
(WHO SAYS I CAN'T HAVE A PART DEUX?)

TENET NINE
Know your Sweet-Spot Time-of-Day

Once upon a time . . .

They moved the meeting to 2:00 p.m. I thought to myself,
"This is never going to work for me." But, because of other
scheduling snafus and preferences, the team decided we would
try it for a while. There I sat in my first meeting at 2:00 p.m.—
partly ready to go to sleep. Partly ready to punch someone
in the face. No part of me was ready for a meeting where we
would make creative decisions.

I barely made it through that first ninety-minute 2:00 p.m.
meeting. I yawned every three minutes. Big, ugly yawns. I
looked like an oxygen-deprived, awkward, full-grown baby
man—rubbing my eyes and desperately craving the fetal
position and a pillow.

Week two was even worse.

By week three, I was ready to hang up my entire career and
murder someone on the way out.

We always generated an agenda at the beginning of these
meetings so at the beginning of week four, when it was time
to hear my agenda ideas, I said (very loudly): "I can't take it
anymore. I hate this meeting time and I'm slowly dying on the
inside."

Everyone laughed. Someone said, "Amen." Come to find out,
everyone in the room hated the meeting time. Passionately. I'm
glad we had this little talk.

Circadian rhythm is the magical, internal clock that is
constantly running in your brain. This magnificent (and often,
seemingly, maleficent) 24-hour internal regulator cycles the

tent you live in between sleepy times and alert times. You can mess with and manipulate your circadian rhythm for a time, but it will rise up to slap you right across your droopy face. Food, exercise, light, lack of light, sound, pace . . . they can all affect your circadian rhythm. And, while your rhythm may change throughout the years, your body is constantly talking to you and letting you know when it's time to be alert and when it's time to go to sleep.

As far as I understand it, while everyone's rhythm differs, most healthy humans sleep when it's dark and wake when it's light. When it's dark outside, your body releases melatonin, and that magical substance that I know nothing of makes you sleepy.

When I lived in Michigan, I had a lot of friends that worked during the night and slept during the day. But, none of them lasted long with that shift. Humans seem to have an innate, sleep-at-night thing going on.

I can hear young folks saying, "I can stay up all night!" I can hear the old folks saying, "I could sleep all day!" True. Age and your own personal need for sleep mess with circadian rhythm. Bottom line, you need sleep, and your body has a natural drum beat by which you march and rest.

I'm not a scientist. But, I don't have to be one to know my own body.

2:00 p.m. meetings suck for me. The majority of healthy humans of all ages feel the post-lunch energy drain in the middle of the day between one-ish and three-ish. 2:00 p.m. is smack dab in the middle of the worst time of day for the bulk of humankind to be creative.

When do you feel energetic? Alive? Fresh? Productive?

Whenever that time is, that's the time you need to set aside to work on your ideas.

Did you notice I said, "set aside?"

Idea Mentalists identify their sweet-spot time-of-day and schedule their creative time in those hours. Painters, musicians, artists, graphic designers, interior designers, business owners, housewives, househusbands, baristas, videographers, dancers, entrepreneurs, and every kid who ever had a lemonade stand, anyone who ever thought they could be famous, anyone who once made a spaceship out of a cardboard box . . . I'm talking to you.

TENET TEN
Believe You are Creative

In Chapter Two, I said, "You have a certain you-ness that no one has." I really believe this. But it doesn't matter what I think. What matters is that YOU think it.

I could write a whole book on this thought above, but, for fear of waxing eloquent, I will keep it short.

My wife has a saying that bothers me. It's okay, she knows. Sometimes, when I say, "That's an awesome idea," she puts on her Debbie Downer voice and says, "Yeahhhhh. I have some good ideas every once in a while." What bothers me about this scene (when it happens) is my wife is one of the most creative Idea Mentalists I know. But, I know her story well enough to know how she had to fight her own demons and outside negative influences to get there (and how she has to fight to stay there). When she puts on this tone, it reminds me that there is still someone inside of her that is fighting insecurity. Not matching up. Feelings of inferiority.

The old insecurity voices that try to beat you down are assholes.

When those voices are silenced in my wife (as they most often are), she is a freaking Mad Scientist of Ideas. She builds, repurposes, salvages, paints, draws, brainstorms, and works harder than most humans I know.

And, she has a brand. She creates things and dreams up things that are unique to her. Sometimes building on others' ideas. But, unique to her.

People want what YOU have to offer.

Do you believe it?

TENET ELEVEN
Exercise Your Belief Muscle

"Who said I have to make a list of an even ten?"

If you don't believe you are creative, it will be harder for you to master what we are calling *becoming an Idea Mentalist*. So, trust me . . . you might not be *that* kind of creative. You may not be *her* kind of creative. But, you are certainly *your* kind. Your kind of creativity counts.

What's the easiest way to silence the old voices? Create. Implement. The more you do, the more you will become familiar and confident with your own brand. Your likes and dislikes. The things you do really well. And, as you master those things, people will take notice. They will want *your* brand of idea to help them move forward.

But, you have to believe it. Belief is necessary to the whole process.

Some of us are paralyzed with feelings of inferiority and need a place to start building our own confidence. Sound about right? Here's a small list of suggestions for you:

Start small. Yes, you want to be a mover and shaker. I get it. You want your ideas to rock the world. You want big ad firms to hire you. You want stages to host you. You want people to frequent your business from all over the world. Books to be written about you. Okay. Me too. But start small. Before dropping a few hundred grand on a national marketing campaign, try taking out social media ads in your area. Start a street-level marketing strategy and invite your friends to cheerlead your ideas.

Think local. I've met many folks who once upon a time were cranking out ideas with hopes of national notoriety and fame. It's great if you desire that kind of a platform. Many of them had their hopes and dreams dashed because the competition and criticism of the national economy is fierce. I've found the local scene to be much more accepting of ideas, and more gracious and tolerant of un-honed ideas. That doesn't mean we should do shoddy work or give up. Always do your best. As you continue to do your best on a local level where people are more likely to be interested and gain trust in you and your brand, your assurance will blossom. People *may* need your ideas in another country, but so do your neighbors. Spend time honing your ideas and strengthening your confidence by investing in the place you live.

Meet the need. Sometimes, people have a *thing* they do real well. And, if they believe the world doesn't need that *thing,* they become reclusive and bitter. It is true that businesses and projects have personalities, and your *thing* may not fit. But, you also have other *things*. Stretch. I haven't met anyone who is truly an Idea Mentalist who has only been gifted with one super-power. Sometimes your *thing* may rhyme with another thing that is needed. But, don't just wait for the opportunities to come knocking where your *thing* is the perfect fit. Asking, "How can I be of help?" is a great way to exercise other muscles that grow confidence, increase blessing, fuel joy, and sharpen us.

Pay attention and practice. At any given time, there are conferences, virtual gatherings, meetups, retreats, gallery events, and seminars where people will gather to share their ideas and their stories. Watch for them. Seek them out. Go to them. Learn from them. Then, put the wisdom you glean into practice

Mentor. Apprentices need Jedi Masters. In one of my favorite movies—*Mr. Holland's Opus*—Richard Dreyfuss' character chased the dream of creating a *great work* but realized at the end of his career that his *greatest work* was in the lives he changed along the way. With all his faults, Mr. Holland was a mentor (even if he didn't know it). *He almost lost his family and his sanity before his awakening. We should all take a lesson from him. People matter. Family matters.*

Investing in *people* continues to be the best investment you can ever make. Others WILL be influenced and mentored by something or someone. It should be you. While investing in other humans is valiant and *enough*, it also has collateral and residual benefits for the mentor. Apprentices and protégés often lack the inhibitions we have and are eager to learn. Their eagerness often lights a fire under us.

If you don't feel like a Master right now, you will. I had a protégé once who has since become a very successful leader in his field. When he was young, he made a ton of mistakes but had an unwavering energy and determination about him that made me want to do better. Think better. Work harder. Invest more. Because he wanted to learn so bad, I wanted to be around him and teach him. One day, while we were working on a project together, he stopped and looked at me and said, "I

can wrap up your whole philosophy in two sentences." Eager
to hear his observations, I gave him my full attention. "What
is it?" I asked. He replied, "You make shit. And, you make shit
happen." I'll take that.

TENET TWELVE
Kill Sacred Cows a.k.a. Moothanasia

The term *sacred cow* comes from the place of honor held by
cows in Hinduism because of their status as mothers and life-
sustaining milk givers. In the majority of Indian states, it is
illegal to eat or possess beef.

The idiom "sacred cow" stems from Hinduism, but figuratively
refers to something that is exempt from analysis or the idea
of change. Sacred cows are those things that exist because
they've always been there, people like them (or, at least it's
what they've become accustomed to), and you shouldn't dare
suggest they be eliminated. Sacred cows are those things that
people get unreasonably uptight about when you suggest they
be changed or done away with.

There are a bunch of reasons why people and systems have and
protect sacred cows:

Some people don't like change.
Good memories can be attached to whatever is in question.
Once upon a time, someone worthy of respect initiated
whatever is being critiqued.
There may be some sentiment of patriotism associated with the
item or idea.
The system or object may have religious significance to
someone.
Nostalgia is a strong emotion.
It's always been said that changing will cost too much money.
Some people and system protectors are just stubborn and refuse
to listen to new ideas.

People fear the potential backlash to the change.
Something has become iconic or part of the aesthetic.

"That piece of art has been hanging there forever. You can't move it unless you want to make people angry. It's a sacred cow around here."

"There's no way they will want to change the seating arrangement in this church at Christmas. It's been like that for years. It's a sacred cow around here."

"Good luck trying to go to a digital receipt filing system. The auditors have always preferred actual paper receipts. It's a sacred cow around here."

These are all real examples from my life. Just for fun, think of three sacred cows from your own experience:

1. _____
2. _____
3. _____

Curious . . . are the things you came up with things you identify in someone or something else, OR are they things you identify *in your own life?* It's harder to identify the sacred cows we protect within our own souls.

Idea Mentalists must be able to feel no remorse for killing sacred cows and they need to learn how to lead people through the process of proper burial.

Let me acknowledge that killing sacred cows can be extremely painful. You might lose friends. Some people will never forgive you. Some will write you off as insensitive. Sounds exciting, doesn't it?! *(As I was proofreading this paragraph, I noticed I accidentally spelled the word "exciting" wrong and originally had the word "exiting." I laughed and said,*

"Paging Dr. Freud," out loud. My little Freudian slip could not have been more revealing. I have in fact been asked to exit an organization for killing sacred cows and it was one of the most painful experiences of my life).

In Chapter Three, we acknowledged "Everything is a Metaphor for Something," and I told you the story about Nick and the "big clunky desk." If you don't remember the story, go back and review it. There are some good examples in there about how one might kill a sacred cow and lead others through a proper mourning.

I have a friend who says, "Behind all traditions are the ashes of logic." In other words, that *thing* or that *system* made sense once upon a time to someone. Even though it makes no sense now. Times change, technology changes, people change, economies change, landscapes change, corporations change, aesthetics change . . . and sometimes those changes necessitate other changes. Sometimes, for the Idea Mentalist to even conceive of an idea, they need to have a solid "no cow is sacred" mentality and trajectory.

How do you identify sacred cows? Sometimes you find out and get surprised when you try to tip them over. Sometimes, someone gives you the heads-up *just in case* you have any wild ideas. Other times you just . . . know.

When *must* they die? When *must* you silence their deafening moos?

When they no longer make any sense.
When there is a bigger "yes" that necessitates you saying "no."
When it's better for humanity.

When it's better for the overall organization and people who work there.

When they no longer help you achieve your mission.
When they contradict your mission, values, and/or strategy.
When they take up space and/or energy that can be better used or spent.
When they are a financial drain with no actual or perceived return.
And sometimes . . . just to set a standard that says, "We will never have sacred cows."

New ideas don't always simply *complement* old ones. New ideas often *replace* old ones. Old ones that are dead. Old ones that are incontinent and make a mess of everything. Old ones that operate as a tail that wags the dog. Old ones that need a resurrection.

The fact remains, everything must die to live again.

If you don't believe aversion or opposition to change can kill you, read the book *Losing the Signal: The Untold Story Behind the Extraordinary Rise and Spectacular Fall of Blackberry* by Jacquie McNish. If you want, you can read the whole thing on your iPhone (chuckle chuckle).

If we don't make change, change will happen to us. And upon us. In spite of us. Without care for us.

Now, how to lead people through the slaughter . . .

Feedforward is your friend. Leak information about what you are thinking of doing with trusted confidants who will help you devise a communication plan, vet the strategy, and spread good cheer once you pull out your sword.

Get in the habit of anticipating controversy. This is also a good impetus to involve comrades in the feedforward process.

Let them give you the word on the street. Let them remind you of that one guy who has that certain opinion. Surface the controversy before it hits you unawares.

Examine the actual and perceived value of the old and the new. What does the new idea contribute? Be able to articulate the ways the new idea is beneficial and distinctively better than the idea you have to kill in order to enact it. Anticipate that perceived value of the old. The way the old looks, feels, reminds, etc., is powerful and hard to overcome. Do your homework. Remember, there's an old saying that goes, "People don't care how much you know until they know how much you care." Don't just dismiss the old ways by calling them dumb. Call attention to the fact they once made sense, but they don't any longer.

Empower the naysayers to become cheerleaders. Give them ownership. Ask them for ways to improve upon the new thing you are proposing. Let them know you aren't afraid of change either.

Mourn the old ways. *But, not for long.* It's okay to cry a little over the sacred cow. Give people some room and time for tears. But not too much. Letting the mourning process go *too long* creates division, distraction, disengagement, detachment, deconstruction, disenfranchisement, and a whole lot of other things that start with "D." Agree on a mourning period, then catch people up to speed and invite them to be a cheerleader of the new as soon as possible. If the mourning goes on for too long and you are in charge, it's your fault. Too much mourning becomes insubordination and bad behavior after a while. There might need to be a *poop or get off the pot moment* for naysayers.

Bring the Old Guard on board as soon as possible. If you know you are anticipating a sacred offering to the god of change and introducing new ideas, bring the *Protectors of the*

Longstanding into your world. As early as possible. Let them help you make change and realize on their own that something has to be done about the old.

PS, this doesn't always work. Every once in a while, someone digs their heels into the earth before reaching the fallow ground. But the risk is worth the reward if you can eliminate bad blood early on and create buy-in with your toughest critics. Then, knight this Old Guard as *Originators of the Way Forward.* Celebrate them. Acknowledge their sacrifice and reward them for breaking molds and sun-setting the old.

Change for the sake of change. This may be the most important precursor to the putting down of sacred cows. People are sometimes fond of saying, "If it ain't broke, don't fix it." Those same voices often say, "Don't change for the sake of change, have a good reason." They are filthy liars and the enemies of forward movement and ideas. If you want to create an environment in your organization or your own consciousness that is ripe for new ideas, change *often.* Everything. Just because. Paint walls. Eat differently. Go somewhere different for vacation. Dress differently. Buy a new hat. Reinvent yourself. Change the flooring. Whatever. Just change. Changing things up *just because* creates a setting and a psyche that is ripe for change. The goal is to create space where people expect and look forward to changing.

When I started a new job in Northern California, some folks on staff bitched and moaned that I painted the walls new colors. A few times. In my first two years. They didn't like how I rearranged the furniture. They didn't understand why I constantly changed out the art installations. I moved the Barista Bar to different areas. I did things they didn't expect, like host live musicians in the lobby. My goal was for guests to experience something new each time they stepped on the campus.

One of my favorite moments came in year two, when one of the naysayers on staff asked me when I was going to change up the art on one of the walls because ". . . it had been there awhile." The fact is it had only been there about six weeks. But, before I started making these *changes for the sake of change*, that wall had previously stayed the same for . . . you guessed it . . . *years*.

Change for the sake of change helps shape a culture that is ready for new things and more readily notices things that become stale and uninteresting.

TENET THIRTEEN
Great Ideas are Indigenous

As I write this section, I'm sitting in a coffee shop in the town of Fair Oaks, California. Fair Oaks is roughly fifteen miles outside of the heart of Sacramento. Fair Oaks has a mix of suburban and semi-rural neighborhoods—in other words, some houses have more land and feel countrified while houses right down the street are tract homes. The American River outlines the south side of the city along with the city of Rancho Cordova. The north, east, and west sides are bordered by three other cities.

The coffee shop I'm in is located in what they call Old Fair Oaks Village. The Fair Oaks Veterans Memorial Amphitheater in the heart of The Village is one of the last surviving outdoor venues offering live theater in the Sacramento area. It's attached to a park in the very center of The Village that is shaded throughout the day with huge, gorgeous trees that fill the rest of the town as well.

Old timers are out riding their bikes today. Couples are walking hand in hand and laughing together. A dog with a head the size of my torso is sitting next to me, and children are gawking at it and getting out of their seats to pet it.

I come here often. It's quaint and artistic. The people are real, and life seems to slow down here. There are plenty of good locally owned restaurants boasting farm-to-fork fare and a local brew pub with some pretty fantastic beers.

But, I haven't even got to the best part of Fair Oaks yet.

It's the *chickens*.

Roaming freely through the streets of Fair Oaks are approximately 200 chickens. (I looked it up. I didn't count them.) The feral fowl have been there for at least three decades according to the locals. They greet you at your car. They eat dinner next to you when you dine outside. They have the right of way on the streets. Roosters and hens alike.

Some tell a story of the chicken population being traced to one man who still lives in the area. There's an old story about a hen who used to lay a daily egg in a planter box and a local resident would crack the egg in his beer every day. Some tell stories about their kids competing for playground space with the chickens. People pose for photos with the feathered local features constantly. The chickens are a big deal and so are the stories surrounding them. Most love them. Some hate them.

But, there's no denying that the makeup of The Village is influenced by the chickens at this point in history. The local artwork, the icons on the business logos, the names of stores and restaurants—chicken stuff.

What does this have to do with ideas?

Imagine, if you will, a couple visiting Fair Oaks and living the experience I just outlined. They leave Fair Oaks after a beer at the Fair Oaks Brew Pub (the one with the rooster in its logo) and on the way home, one turns to the other and says, "That city really has a great thing going. We ought to introduce chickens into our city." So, they go home and buy a few chickens hoping to *organically* introduce them to their city of San Jose—the "Capital of the Silicon Valley"—home to Zoom, Cisco Systems, Apple, Google, Yahoo, Intel, eBay, and others. Home of crazy traffic. Home of the $2 million, two-bedroom home.

It doesn't take much imagination to picture what a huge disaster this would be. Square peg. Round hole. Horrible idea. They'd probably get fined or thrown in jail.

Yet every single day, people introduce ideas or tweaks of ideas to their environments without a thought to how it makes no sense for the environment they live and work in. Too often, ideas are copied, reproduced, reinvented, and regurgitated into environments where the idea just doesn't work. Many of us see the idea's demise before it's officially launched.

We lived in Michigan for over a decade. The downtown area of our town's depressed blue-collar economy was a revolving door of business ideas. And while people struggled to survive and find gainful employment, storefronts popped up regularly offering such goods as balloons and flowers—items that you could buy for half the price at the local supermarket. The only things that thrived no matter how many stores were opened in our town were cigarettes and booze.

Indigenous ideas are ideas that make sense with who you are and where you live—be that local, regional, or global.

Indigenous ideas are those that flow from your own story and experience.

Indigenous ideas are believable.

Indigenous ideas have an innate energy and surface enthusiasm. They are contagious and inspiring. People are willing to take risks for something that sounds believable.

Indigenous ideas never assume that because it worked *over there* it will work *here*.

Indigenous ideas make sense because of who you are, where you live, and what is needed. They are filled with imagination that comes from knowing your culture and reading the signs around you. They are the kind of ideas that make people sit back and say, "Why didn't I think of this?" Or, "I thought of this before and never pulled the trigger."

Indigenous ideas don't have to be *sold* as much as they need to be *celebrated* by someone who can tell a story well and surface the need to listen. Show me someone who lights themselves on fire for what they believe, and I'll show you people following them and buying their products and/or ideas. No one likes a pushy salesman who doesn't even believe in what they are offering. And, you can't manufacture belief in your idea. It has to come from deep inside. If it's not indigenous, it will come across as disingenuous.

Of course, some ideas are not simply *locally* indigenous. Some are regional or global. But before an idea is launched for any organization or market, local or far and wide, one *has* to ask if it makes sense for the market it's being introduced to. You'd think it would be an easy question. And still, in Michigan, I saw three overpriced and poorly executed burrito restaurants go into the same exact building over a period of ten years. Followed by the balloon store.

TENET FOURTEEN
There's Always an Exception

Just like there's always an OPTION C, there's always an exception to conventional wisdom. But, buyer beware, there is usually a steep cost to the exception, and it doesn't always work. The Idea Mentalist has to determine if the idea is worth the risk of taking on conventional wisdom in a fight to the finish. Sometimes, a lesson is learned. Sometimes, the rewards are beautiful. And, guaranteed, the rewards are always superseded by *love motivation*. I'll explain . . .

The first huge chunk of money I lost on an idea was in 2007—two years after the launch of YouTube. For two years, people had been watching low-quality videos made with handheld cameras and the iPhone that had been introduced to the market one year earlier. My idea? To start a company offering innovative educational segments that were rich in metaphor and taught about the human spirit in five minutes or less. All with hand-held cameras. Guerilla films. Low budget. Lo-fi. I sold my friend Michael on the idea to join me as an equal partner in the venture. We called the video shorts *5-Minute Thought Grenades* and we named our company Popnovella. Pop was short for popular, as in pop music. A novella is a short story.

Conventional wisdom said the market was flooded with free videos and people would *not* be willing to pay for mine. At least, not without any extra perks and incentives.

Conventional wisdom said the iPhone was starting to revolutionize the way we make videos in a world where everyone is a movie maker and producer.

In this case . . . conventional wisdom was right. I paid the price.

I sat with one executive after another that marketed short films. They all told me I had a great idea—as long as it didn't cost them any money. Some were willing to market my company for a fee as I leveraged their market, but no one wanted to put any energy behind it. They loved my stories and metaphors. They loved the concept of 5-*Minute Thought Grenades*. But, not enough to give me money or even hype the product.

I had the balls to believe my own internet platform was enough to market the product. People liked what I had to say. I spoke at conferences on *innovation,* for crying out loud.
So, I sallied forth. Spending thousands of hours. And thousands of dollars. Not a lifetime's savings by any means. But, for someone who didn't have any money and lived from paycheck to paycheck, it was a fortune.

Not only did I ignore conventional wisdom—the market was changing, and people were getting used to getting things for free—, I ignored what was happening in the way people were viewing all their content. I chose to put the films on a dying piece of plastic. The DVD. In the world of education, we were entering a time where no one was interested in buying DVDs anymore. There was already just too much content on the internet. For free.

To be honest, I had been making films like this for a long time. Way before I started a company. For fun. And, to share with various organizations I was a part of. To inspire them. My visions of grandeur got the best of me, and I ignored some pretty important signs the market was screaming at me.

Maybe I could have reinvented the idea in light of my revelations and empty bank account. But I lost courage. I got tired. I lost hope. And, I was embarrassed.

Here's what really killed me: Somewhere along the line, amidst the hustle and disappointments, I also *lost my love for the craft.* It was getting harder and harder to come up with rich metaphors and clever scripts. My motivation changed and my energy waned. It would be years before I wanted to make another video about anything.

One of the key ingredients for being the only salmon swimming downstream in the river of conventional wisdom is to be absolutely sure of your *motivation.* I'm quite certain that part of your motivation has to be *an innate love* for the thing. Whatever your thing is. It's the *love for the thing* that breaks down walls, wows people, wins people over, and surfaces a need to pay attention. It's your love for the thing that creates new markets and silences the naysayers. And sometimes, that love for the thing covers a multitude of conventional wisdom sins and ends up breaking the mold.

But, *love for the thing* alone is not always enough.

"Find something you love to do and then find a way to get paid for it," someone once told me (I mentioned that earlier). It's really good wisdom. But, it's *proverbial.* Proverbs are things that are true about life much of the time, but not all of the time. Proverbs are not promises. Sometimes you love something very much, and when it turns the corner and becomes something you *need to do* to survive, you can grow to despise it.

My friends David and Ally are photographers. Really good ones. You'd think that in a world where people carry around a personal photography studio in their hands, with cameras more powerful and sharper than any camera their parents ever owned (or, at least the same quality for a portion of the price), that David and Ally would be out of business by now.

But they're not. They're kicking it in the shorts. They're growing.

David and Ally *love what they do*. That's the first part of their magic equation for success. They would be taking copious amounts of photos in their spare time if they worked other jobs. They love the art.

However, they've learned along the way *that love for the thing* alone can become tedious, taxing, and lose all its *joie de vivre*.

To keep their love for the art a high priority, they have found ways to incorporate other things they love into their photography and build a thriving business—namely, *travel* and *spending time with people*.

McKay Photography Academy offers trip-of-a-lifetime photography tours across the globe and continuing education classes out of their home base near Sacramento, California. They sell photography expertise for sure, but what they really sell is *adventure. Friendship. Community. Experience.* Oftentimes my wife and I have thought about going out to dinner with our friends only to remember they are on a tour. "Was it Croatia, Tanzania, or Mongolia?"

Conventional wisdom says that everyone is a photographer. Conventional wisdom says, "My iPhone camera can beat up your dad's clunky camera." Conventional wisdom says, "Wait . . . people still get portraits taken?" But David and Ally have found the exception.

Their exception is motivated by love.

Coupled with other mutual loves.

And an insatiable drive to see others succeed.

They seem unstoppable.

In 2016, David published his first book, *Photography*

Demystified, that went on to be a bestseller on Amazon. Conventional wisdom says, "Don't give all your ideas away or your business will fail." But, he sold a pile of these books— not to mention the book he also wrote for kids with the same approach.

David is an Idea Mentalist. I have sat in a car with him on long drives many times as we talk about ideas. Some of his ideas are so great, I want to steal them. But, he trusts me with them and he's my friend, so I keep them inside.

TENET FIFTEEN
Be Motivated by a Love for Ideas

We said something like this above, but I want to drive this point home. The most fulfilled people I know are Idea Mentalists who are in it for the thrill of the hunt. The scent of a new idea. The allure of the adventure.

Oftentimes, when new ideas and innovations are being pursued, opportunity comes knocking. I can tell you from personal experience that opportunity knocking on your door can bring an unparalleled sense of accomplishment in comparison to killing yourself in pursuit of recognition and success.

The first time I realized this, I was at a conference for artists in Nashville, Tennessee, in February of 2007. Twitter had just come on the scene a few months earlier in July of 2006, but it hadn't gained much in popularity. I was a moderator for a breakout session and had a Twitter account because one of my early-adopter friends, David Buchanan, had turned me on to it. I thought it would be super fun to get everyone in our session set up with a Twitter account and put our live Twitter feed on the screen while the speaker was talking so we could interact with one another. It was a huge hit.

I ended up bringing the concept back to the church I was working with. For a couple of months, whenever we gathered in a large space, I put the Twitter feed on the screen, and we interacted with one another. Some people hated the idea at first, but it caught on—especially after we held classes to help people understand, use, and embrace Twitter as a legit communication vehicle. It was new. It was undiscovered. It was interactive and participatory. And, way different than anything we had done on screen in the past.

Soon, word spread about my little experiment. People started blogging about it. I started getting calls about how to harness the power of social media in the context of a meeting. Then, TIME magazine called. They wanted to come interview me about how we were using this new technology application in our environment. I couldn't be in town when they wanted to interview me, but they came out and interviewed my colleagues. What was super fun for me is that some of my colleagues hated the idea of Twitter at first, but became cheerleaders when they saw the idea in action and the buzz it was creating.

Finally, in June 2009—three years after the introduction of Twitter and two years after my first experiment—our article appeared in TIME magazine with Michelle Obama on the cover.

There was absolutely no pay for this. No money came my way for the idea. It was the love of the thing that motivated me. The thrill of new ideas. The interaction with people. The buzz of meeting new people and doing things I had never done. Money never crossed my mind.

Then, a publishing house called. And, I wrote a book. That led to a second book with them. That led to numerous conferences as a guest speaker. That led to me meeting and spending time with some of my heroes. And new experiences. And more beautiful people.

One tiny little notion to introduce something that was a bit outside everyone's comfort zone continues to shape my life in new ways and create new opportunities and new ideas in ways I never imagined.

TENET SIXTEEN
The Fast Eat the Slow and Everything is Going Faster

Earlier, I mentioned the HBO show *Silicon Valley*. It's a hilariously inappropriate view into the life of startup companies in Silicon Valley. If there's one thing this show highlights that is a completely different economy of ideas than the world I grew up in, it's the concept of the *fast eating the slow*.

Long ago, in an Idea Galaxy far, far away, big companies would swallow up little companies in the business world. If Little Company A had a great idea and not a lot of capital, Big Company B would eat it up. Yum yum. That was in the days of brick and mortar. The big ate the small. The strong ate the weak.

Not anymore.

Speed is now the competitive edge with new ideas. The little guy with the big idea who moves fast soon finds himself outpacing the competition. The scrawny weakling can find themselves ahead of the giant ominous mogul if they are willing to run faster. This is great news for the weaker guy who is used to getting chased by the bully. In this new economy, ideas are the weapons of the future. And, the bullies have no foothold.

This concept works hand-in-hand with incubating and graduating, like we talked about in Chapter Three. Sometimes, in order to move fast and make your idea known before someone else does, it requires a little bit of ready-fire-aim.

It's not uncommon (as a matter of fact it's a recurring trope) for the characters on the show, *Silicon Valley,* to have an incredible idea but not move fast enough before either the technology changes or their idea is leaked to another who improves upon and launches their idea first. The show does a great job of leading us to believe this is exactly what happens every day in the real Silicon Valley. And, it's not that far-fetched. We know technology has a diminishing shelf life.

In the fast-paced changing tech world, ideas need to be enacted quickly, not only because someone else might act faster but also because the idea may no longer be viable around the next corner.

For kicks and giggles (and to have your mind blown), read the book *The Singularity is Near* by author, speaker, entrepreneur, scientist, and futurist Ray Kurzweil. One of the smartest humans ever, Kurzweil has the ability to communicate top-shelf ideas to the commoner like myself. Right off the bat in the Prologue, Kurzweil says:

> . . . I remain convinced of this basic philosophy: no matter what quandaries we face—business problems, health issues, relationship difficulties, as well as the great, scientific, social, and cultural challenges of our time—there is an idea that can help us all prevail. Furthermore, we can find that idea. And when we find it, we need to implement it. My life has been shaped by this imperative. The power of an idea—this is itself an idea.

Kurzweil makes a very convincing case that in the tech world, if it feels like technology is rapidly expanding at an alarming rate, it's because it actually is. Kurzweil defines this as the "Law of Accelerating Returns"—where the ideas and understanding of today is building upon the ideas and understanding of the past so that human understanding is on an exponential growth curve as opposed to a linear growth pattern. Kurzweil says about this exponential growth:

> . . . we won't experience one hundred years of technological advance in the twenty-first century; we will witness on the order of twenty thousand years of progress . . . or about one thousand times greater than what was achieved in the twentieth century. (Kurzweil 2005, 11)

"Well, my ideas aren't tech ideas," you might say to yourself. Understandable. But, I'm convinced every organization, business, family structure, church, or whatever your sphere of influence is both directly and indirectly affected by technology and human understanding. We don't have to live and work in the tech world (computers, robots, AI) to be impacted by advances in those areas. Acting fast on ideas in a rapidly changing world sets us up for success in the future as changes happen to us.

Once upon a time, I led music in my local church. When I first started doing this, my wife helped me by flipping transparencies of song lyrics on an overhead projector so that our congregation could see words on a screen (I just dated myself). She was the only one I trusted in this role because novices would put things on the projector upside down and/or backwards every single time. Transparencies weren't ideal, but they were the advanced technology of the time. Some churches even considered you a bit rebellious if you used overhead transparencies instead of hymnals. After all, hand-held hymnals had been a tradition for hundreds of years.

I was frustrated by transparencies. Unless I made them myself, few of them had matching font sizes or even font styles. They seldom had poetic flow. Sometimes, people split the lines we were supposed to sing in weird places. They were boring to look at as well. I remember having a "crazy" idea to call together a group of artists to design overhead transparencies so that they didn't look so sterile on the screen. Some said it would be distracting. Some said it was unnecessary. But, *who said we can't make transparencies engaging?*

We launched a new chapter for song transparencies. Artists would photocopy existing works of their own art on the transparencies as well as use pens to add panache to the transparencies. Artistic song transparencies led to speakers wanting to create beautiful works of art for their teaching. This seems so humorous now in a world with PowerPoint, Keynote, and other presentation software.

When I started designing these with artists, someone suggested to me I had hit a gold mine. "Imagine if you sold these pieces of art to churches all over the world? People will eat this stuff up!" I toyed with the idea for a while but decided not to make a move.

In all honesty, I might have made a killing had I acted upon that idea right away. And, that idea would have revolutionized the church music world. For about a minute. Until we all got computers and employed projectors with thousands of lumens that projected moving video backdrops to lyrics. This was only thirty years ago.

I didn't launch a transparency business. But, I did build a team of artists that bought into the idea of creating beautiful transparencies to enhance the experience for our people. And it was so worth it. Here's another great thing about acting fast on ideas: even though the technology changed overnight, rendering transparencies useless, the work I had done to build a solid team of artists who had freedom to create works of beauty laid the foundation for them to transfer that idea to new technology and create works of digital art.

The early work we did in the world of cumbersome transparencies built a camaraderie and trust among the artists. We began to dream of other ways to employ artists and create rich experiences. In a world where art was sometimes seen as suspect, or simply something to be leveraged for marketing, we created a world where art was an integral part of an experience and a beautiful way to tell a story. Visual art, performance art, art galleries, pop-up galleries, and live painting and musical experiences became standard for our church community. While this might be more commonplace in some church circles today, it was almost unheard of thirty years ago.

Everything I learned in the early days about building teams of artists and involving them in the process of creating experiences has not only proven helpful for my own communities but has also given me a platform to be able to inspire and coach others to do the same within their communities. And, I get paid for my expertise.

The rate of change is rapidly accelerating, not only in the tech world but everywhere. The Idea Mentalist understands that acting fast on ideas—no matter the environment and economy—doesn't return void. That is, when they understand that *experience* is also mounting and exponential. The ideas you have today, when acted upon, will lay the groundwork for future ideas as you build upon your growing knowledge, tools you've developed, and application of all the lessons learned in previous ideations.

TENET SEVENTEEN
You're Not Allowed to Be Bored

This was a rule in our home growing up. I passed it on to my kids. I've heard my daughter repeat the same thing to her kids.

The thought behind this is, there's plenty to do and you can use your imagination to create your own engaging activity. The Idea Mentalist will certainly be weary from time to time because we're human. But they can't reside in a world of boredom.

When we're tired and/or relaxed, we don't need much to keep us entertained. Boredom sets in during the times when our minds and bodies are racing at full throttle, and we can't find anything to satisfy our stimulation.

Truth be told, I seldom get bored the older I get—not simply because I've finally found ways to curtail my boredom, but because I tire more easily. When we were young, my wife and I would see older couples in restaurants eating without speaking a word to each other. Staring into space. We used to hold hands and stare at each other with rainbows and butterflies over our heads and say, "How sad. We don't ever want to be like that. Let's make sure we stay in love." Now that we're older, we know there was nothing wrong with those couples. They were very much in love. They were just tired. (That's our little joke. It's not always true.)

It's important for Idea Mentalists to stay strong, healthy, fit, hydrated, and well-nourished to stay sharp. No matter what stage of life you're in.

Strong, healthy, fit, hydrated, and well-nourished aren't simply adjectives that refer to our physical bodies. They also apply to our minds. Our spiritual state. Our mental state. In order to nourish these things, we need a steady diet of mind food. Spirit food. Soul food.

One thing I've learned throughout the years is that we are all shaped differently when it comes to the things that actually work to feed us. For years, I was told I needed to go to a steady diet of conferences to help me stay nourished. It wasn't until

I was in my forties that I felt the permission to say, "I hate conferences." Conferences usually leave me wanting, fidgety, disagreeable, and feeling like I just want to leave and get to work.

Writing music, listening to music, going to concerts, listening to podcasts, volunteering, entertaining, reading, camping, nature walks, watching documentaries, audiobooks, watching movies, trying new coffee shops, job shadowing people, hearing people's stories, having coffee with entrepreneurs . . . these are all things that feed my spirit.

You need to find your own soundtrack. Your own jam. But, find one.

The Idea Mentalist finds a way to fully engage in activities that feed the spirit without feeling guilty for not working. At the same time, they find a rhythm in their play that allows them to be observant and leverage their play towards their ideas. In everything they do, they are making lists, taking notes, connecting dots, allowing their minds to wander, and thinking in metaphor.

Idea Mentalists take time to be still, but reject boredom. They take time to rest, but rally against monotony. They take time to clear their mind, but refuse to be perpetually disconnected.

TENET EIGHTEEN
Creativity Flows from the Positive

I could sum up what I'm about to say in the next few paragraphs by saying, "*Idea Mentalists are not negative people.*" Negative people might have an idea every once in a while. However, in my experience, perpetually negative people eventually drain the life out of the spaces they inhabit and contaminate the creative space of others.

Negative people can really suck. No one wants to be around a negative person. So, we end up not listening to negative people. Everything they say is suspect after a while. We imagine their ideas to be full of manipulation and posturing. It's hard to get past the exterior of a negative person even when they have something interesting to say. They're exhausting.

We all have the potential within us to be negative. I've had both passing periods and extended seasons of negativity in my life. Idea Mentalists fight negativity within themselves and find ways to make their positivity meter spike more often than not. They develop an acute sense for sniffing out negativity in themselves and in their environments and they develop ways to protect themselves from being tainted while exercising grace, hope, peace, inclusion, celebration, and love.

Idea Mentalists realize that everyone is battling something. We all have a story. They practice care and compassion with those around them—even the ones who threaten to spoil their good vibes. This doesn't mean they don't set boundaries. It is often necessary to set up rules and boundaries that don't allow negative people to rain on our parade. Sometimes the negative person needs to be confronted. Or ignored. Or blocked on social media. But, the Idea Mentalist's first thought should always be *love*. Seeking to understand. Desiring to manage conflict.

Idea Mentalists cannot allow themselves to become bitter and angry people. Bitterness and anger change the shape of our faces. Bitterness and anger are the evil pheromones that trigger bad responses in those around us and eventually lead to the breeding out of ideas. So, Idea Mentalists are committed to love, and resolution, and reconciliation.

Pick up any book you want with research on positivity, and you will read about the benefits of longer life, better marriages, contentment in the workplace, lower levels of depression, and fewer instances of discontent and distress. Those are all fantastic realities of positivity.

Idea Mentalists are *perspective* people. They *seek* perspective in every situation. This is not to say that every situation is healthy or that every bit of criticism has some grain of truth—that is simply not true. However, Idea Mentalists are always asking:

"What is the takeaway here?"
"How can I make sure this doesn't happen again?"
"Is there anything I can celebrate here?"
"What can I learn from this?"
"What other things are happening in my life that I can celebrate since this situation sucks?"

This seems like a big duh. Right?

And yet, organizations are full of negative people trying to have the next big idea that will get them noticed or promoted, and full of negative people using power and position to be heard. Every once in a while, they sneak through and beat the system. The rain falls on the just and the unjust. But, proverbially speaking, negative people do not win.

Idea Mentalists create habits that keep them on the track of positivity. They speak positively. They tell their children positive things. They praise their employees. They complement their spouses. They spread good cheer. They write positive social media posts. They don't start or participate in petty arguments on social media. They use beautiful and hopeful adjectives. They expect to wake up and have something great happen to them. They expect to wake up and exalt others.

To Sum It Up

In the last two chapters, we've covered a ton of ground. Eighteen Tenets. I thought you might want a list of the Tenets as bullet points of an Idea Mentalist's philosophy. I personally have some other idiosyncrasies that make up my own personal expanded philosophy, but the ones we listed in the last two chapters are the ones I believe are essential. My personal philosophy will leak out in other parts of this book from here on out. Below are the essentials I believe you need to adopt on your own road to becoming an Idea Mentalist. Refer to this list often. Go back and review often.

IDEA MENTALIST TENETS
- "Who Says We Can't Do That?"
- Break Your Own Rules
- Everything is a Metaphor for Something
- There's Always an OPTION C
- "How?" is the Wrong Question
- It's Easier to Lower the Bar Than to Raise it
- Work Towards Version Four
- Understand Incubating and Graduating
- Find Your Sweet-Spot Time-of-Day
- Believe You are Creative
- Exercise Your Belief Muscle
- Kill Sacred Cows a.k.a. Moothanasia
- Great Ideas are Indigenous
- There's Always an Exception
- Be Motivated by a Love for Ideas
- The Fast Eat the Slow and Everything is Going Faster
- You're Not Allowed to Be Bored
- Creativity Flows from the Positive

PART TWO
THE HABITS OF A MENTALIST

CHAPTER FIVE
EVERYTHING NEW

Practicalosophy

The previous four chapters have been dedicated to what some might call the more "heady" parts of the book—the philosophy, the wisdom, the sagacity of an Idea Mentalist. The remainder of this book is what some might call the *practical* parts of the book.

Only, don't allow yourself to think that way—even though you'll be tempted to. To an Idea Mentalist, the philosophy is necessary and fabric to the practical. The practical is less practical without the practicality of the philosophy. In other words, there are things in the remainder of this book you will want to try on for size to try and stretch your idea muscles. And, you should. But, if you want to become an Idea Mentalist, you need to have an innate *philosophy* that drives your perspective as you experience. A sound philosophy of ideas will cause you to approach the proverbially practical differently and it will leverage your experiences.

It's like this . . .

I love Disneyland. The one in Anaheim, California. We used to go there a lot when I was a kid. It's magical. The old-growth trees in the park, the grasses, the landscape, the architecture, even the smell of Southern California can't be beat. If you're ever there when it rains, the smell of the hot asphalt as the rain splashes on it is intoxicating. The smells of cotton candy, popcorn, corn dogs, and pretzels satiate the air 24/7.

Disneyland is full of vintage icons, like the Matterhorn Bobsleds that are sure to give you bruises, the Dumbo the Flying Elephant ride that you'll wait in line for until your day turns into Tomorrowland, and the annoying-and-yet-somehow-tearful boat ride journey through It's a Small World. At the same time, Disneyland is always updating and expanding. It seems there is always some new thing or updated thing under construction when you visit. And, it's all worth it.

My kids are grown and out of the house now, but when my youngest daughter turned eighteen, I took her to Disneyland. I wanted my princess to turn eighteen in the park. I saved for two years to take her on this special daddy-daughter trip. I made reservations way in advance at the Blue Bayou restaurant—the one you see from the boats inside the Pirates of the Caribbean ride. We spent four consecutive days in the park, and also hopped over to Disney California Adventure every once in a while. We logged 10-13 miles each day for a grand total of forty-five miles of walking over four days. We loved imagining how far we had walked if those miles were in a straight line— for instance, it was like a walk from our town of Folsom into the city of Sacramento and back home again (which seemed like a heck of a long way for us).

When I held my daughter's hand and walked through the park for her very first time (that she could remember—she went as an infant), I started crying. I felt kinda dumb at first as the tears rolled off my beard, but then I embraced it. I wanted to feel all the feels. Cliff Edward's 1940 version of "When You Wish Upon a Star" was playing as we rounded the corner on to Main Street U.S.A. My heart raced a little. I was transported back in time to when I was about five or six years old and stood in the circular hub looking at Sleeping Beauty's castle while getting my photo taken with Donald Duck. My daughter had seen that photo and suggested we recreate the photo forty-ish years later (which we did before we left the park).

She embraced the birthday experience at Disney to its magical magnitude. She wore a button that said it was her birthday. She loved how cast members and guests told her happy birthday all day long. We rode The Many Adventures of Winnie the Pooh over and over again because it's super cute and it has a birthday scene at the end that makes it feel like they are celebrating *you.* Because, in Disneyland, they are. We had a free dessert at the Blue Bayou. We did whatever she wanted. All. Day. Long. Every. Day.

Disneyland doesn't have employees. It has *cast members*. No matter your job, you are a *cast member*. I've known about five people who have worked at the park at one time or another, and they always tell the same story—when you work for Disneyland, you are playing a role. Your job is to make people happy in the happiest place on earth. On the trip with my daughter, I stood in an alley waiting for my daughter to come out of the restroom where she was trying on a Tinkerbell outfit. It happened to be the alley where some characters walked through to take a break or change shifts. I was fortunate enough to have Snow White walk past me. I greeted her as I would any adult with a "Hey, how's it going?" I guess I was expecting her to answer with the obligatory, "Great. Thanks," and be on her enchanted way. But, this *was* Snow White. In a high-pitch voice, she folded her hands up to her chin and said, "I just love your beard! It reminds me of my friend, Grumpy." Then she giggled incessantly as she walked through the magical doors that took her back to reality.

I wanted to follow her. Not in some weird, creepy old man princess-fetish kinda way. I just wanted to be part of her world (yes, I know, that's what Ariel sings). I want to live in a world where princesses giggle, dragons are slain, spells are broken with kisses, and people live happily ever after.

Why am I telling you this story?

Because, when I left for this magical trip, these are a few of the things I heard from friends and acquaintances . . .

"Disney? Oh, God. It's so overpriced."
"That park sure has changed. I'm never going back."
"Good luck getting on any rides."

"Hope you picked a time when the crowds are lower. Our experience there sucked."
"Hope it doesn't rain on you. It ruined our vacation."
"Happiest place on earth, my ass."
"My husband will never go there again."

Without an underlying Idea Mentalist philosophy, the journey for experience and new ideas will be overshadowed by what is seen as superfluous, frustrating, exhausting, and inconvenient.

The Idea Mentalist has a philosophy of ideas that is also just a philosophy of . . . *life*. They see things differently because they imagine themselves as a character in a story. They imagine everyone they meet as playing a potential role in their unique story. They are always asking questions and are curious about everything in every circumstance.

Someone just looking to get some ideas or get inspired *might* take a trip to Disneyland and soak it in—because it's a *practical* thing to do when you are looking for ideas. It's Disney. Duh. They *might* find something that sparks an idea for them. They *might* try a new experience and come away with something that triggers an idea they may not have otherwise had.

But, unless they have a perspective philosophy that *engages with experiences for all they're worth*, they are going to get distracted and derailed. Engaging with every experience is a prerequisite to inspiring ideas.

Soon, they will be annoyed by the rain instead of breathing deeply the scent of it. They will be frustrated by the crowds instead of counting how many people wish them a happy birthday. They will be pissed off every time they lay down another hundred bucks for something that costs half that price at home instead of counting their blessings and being thankful they had the opportunity to save for over two years so they didn't have to stress about the money and just embrace it all carefree. They will make a decision to "never go there again" and choose to be poisoned forever with their bad memories.

Idea Mentalists *cannot* and *will not* live life simply in search of a new idea as they suck the potential ideas out of an experience. They will live in a way that clears their mind to receive another idea as it floats through the air like a familiar melody. They don't see ideas as commodities to be pilfered from an experience, but rather they see experiences— people, work, play, environments, food—as things to be enjoyed *just because*. And, as they engage with the life all around them, they create and cultivate a space for ideas.

Make sense?

With that said, let's talk about some useful—practical, if you must—ways that an Idea Mentalist embraces life. Let's start with the title of this chapter that I'm finally getting to, "Everything New."

Waking and Embracing

I mentioned in the beginning of this book that my favorite restaurant is the one I haven't been to yet. People will ask me occasionally if I have a favorite restaurant, and I always like to give this answer. Because it's true. I mean sure, I have spots I frequent because they have that certain *joie de vivre* that I crave, or that certain blend of coffee, or that certain blueberry scone, or that certain burger, or that certain beer on tap.

(True confessions: I'm writing this part as I sit at a restaurant called El Burro Loco up by Mt. Hood, Oregon. It was new to me three days ago, but I had to come back for the Tacos Al Pastor.)

However, I will surrender my desire to return to one of my favorite haunts 99% of the time in favor of a new restaurant—especially if someone else is experiencing it with me for their first time as well.

(Today, my wife is trying the Tacos Al Pastor for the first time, and I am grinning as I watch her experience them.)

Each day, I have a series of questions I ask myself as soon as my feet hit the floor. It's part of my "Everything New" approach to each day. Each question is framed by an innate belief that the day is going to be fresh, new, and different. It has to be. It's a *new* day. Each new day should bring with it new things. These are my daily questions with a bit of an explanation for each:

Who am I going to meet today?
I love walking into a restaurant in town and being called by name. There is something magical about being known. I figure other people feel the same. So, I try to meet someone new every day. This requires proactivity. I don't assume people will walk up and introduce themselves. I have to ask for their names. I have to engage in conversation. I keep a running list of names of people I meet and notes about them. It's my goal to know every shop owner and employee in every store and restaurant I frequent in my town. Because, these are my people. It's where I live.

What will I be surprised by today?
I expect that I will experience some kind of wonder in the day. This requires paying attention. Asking questions.

What new experience will I create for myself today?
I walk where my feet take me. I take new routes to and from work. I walk into stores I have never been in even if it looks like it's not my flavor or style. I watch movies I've never heard of. I try food I have never ordered before. I listen to radio stations and playlists I have never heard. I take five minutes

to stop at the side of the road and read the historical markers. I walk inside of buildings just because they are there. I take elevators to top floors just because.

What am I going to read today?
Every day, I read something. Anything. Every February, I read nothing but fiction.

What am I going to eat today?
Food is a big deal to me. I cook a lot. My wife cooks a lot. When we eat out, we aim to try a new restaurant. I seldom eat at chains, and when I do, it's usually because I'm outvoted. So, I make the best of it. Plan your food. It's a huge part of your life.

What will I listen to today?
I collect vinyl. There are albums in my stack I have never listened to—they were a gift, I found them cheap, they were recommended, etc. It is a great experience to listen ALL THE WAY through an entire album. Sitting still. I do this as often as possible. When I don't have time to do that in my day, I at least make sure I am listening to something I have never heard before. Music is a language. It speaks louder, deeper, more eloquently, softer, with more conviction, more emotionally, more emotively than any other language. It informs my life.

What am I going to make today?
I make something every day. Period. I design my own thank you notes. I draw. I paint. I build. I craft. I write.

What am I going to imagine today?
I walk with my phone in hand. I take photos of things that inspire me. I talk out loud. I speak my thoughts into the recorder app. I collect notebooks. They are full of notes and ideas. Song lyrics. Quips. Jokes. When I think it, I write it down so I can dig deeper. If I get an idea, I start to flesh it out

with bullet points. I may never do it, but I will do something, and daily imagination is where it starts.

Who am I going to encourage today?
Every day, I send someone a note. An email. A card. Doesn't matter. Every day, SOMEONE will hear some encouraging words from me. I want to be encouraged. I'm sure they do too. So, it breathes life into my day to take two minutes to drop a note.

Where will I spend some personal time today?
On my motorcycle. Spinning vinyl. On a walk. Late at night after everyone's asleep. I need it. It fuels me.

What conversations will I have today?
I try to have a face-to-face appointment every day. I look for excuses to have them spontaneously. I meet folks for coffee. A new conversation with someone every day (that's not work-related, not to troubleshoot, not conflict-resolution) to learn more about them is life-giving.

How will I greet nature today?
I go on walks. I sing to the birds. I stand at my hummingbird feeder for twenty minutes to watch my little friends come greet me. I talk to the cats. I take new trails. I walk at different times of day to literally see things in a different light. I walk in the rain without an umbrella. Sometimes, I let my dogs, Mr. Tumnus and Reepicheep, lead the way as we walk the trails. They're good conversation partners as well.

How will I play today?
I watch movies. I sing songs loudly while walking through the workplace. I play board games. I go for drives. I write songs. I write poems. I tell ridiculous Dad jokes. I talk in accents. I hold laugh parties. I make up stupid games with my staff.

What will God say to me today?

I don't know how you feel about God. Maybe you talk to the Universe. Maybe you refer to a Higher Power. Maybe you don't believe in a God at all. Wherever you're at, I'm describing my experience here, so don't take it as prescriptive for an Idea Mentalist. I believe in God. I don't expect God to audibly call my name. But, I expect God will give me perspective. I expect God is speaking through others and I need to shut up a bit. I expect I'll learn a lesson.

What will I say to God today?
I believe God's listening. You might think it weird, but I think God wants to hear from me. So, I tell God everything. I think God's not afraid of my honesty. I laugh with God. Cry with God. Yell at God. Confess to God. Consult God. Ask things of God. Apologize to God. Ask God for wisdom. Nothing is off-limits.

What will I say yes to today?
"How would you like to go on a drive and meet someone?" **Yes.**
"How would you like to come to work with me and see what I do?" **Yes.**
"How would you like to play music for my gathering?" **Yes.**
"How would you like to come over for dinner?" **Yes.**
"Are you willing to speak to our group?" **Yes**
"Can I introduce you to my friend?" **Yes.**

Recently, my son said to me, "Dad, we've lived a pretty charmed life." I agree. These are legit questions above that have led to some of the most memorable experiences and friendships of my life.

Of course, some things will be routine . . . or will they? I believe even the routine and mundane can and do carry with them a sense of originality if we allow them to and if we pursue it.

The Unusual Routine

I'm so, I'm so sick of this place
I'm so ready for a change of pace
I'm just looking for a new routine
So she spins her globe and the next thing you know
She's living in Liechtenstein

—From *New Routine* by Fountains of Wayne

Cause it's a bittersweet symphony this life Trying to make ends meet, you're a slave to the money then you die. I'll take you down the only road I've ever been down You know the one that takes you to the places where all the veins meet, yeah. No change, I can't change, I can't change, I can't change, But I'm here in my mold, I am here in my mold. But I'm a million different people from one day to the next I can't change my mold, no, no, no, no, no

—From *Bitter Sweet Symphony* by The Verve

The strict definition of *routine* is "a regularly followed sequence of action; a task or tasks performed over and over; a regularly replicated procedure as opposed to something done for a special occasion." Routine in and of itself is not bad. Sometimes it's necessary. *(I want my doctor to follow routine procedures for cleanliness and disinfection if I'm ever receiving open-heart surgery.)*

However, the word *routine* is often relegated to negative connotations in our everyday language—*boring, repetitive, monotonous*. "How was work today, Dave?" "Oh, you know. Same routine."

One of my dad's favorite sayings growing up was, "Another day, another dollar." Sometimes, if you asked him how he was doing, he would say, "Same ol' same ol'." What's weird is that my dad is one of the most fun-loving and spontaneous people you will ever meet. I don't think he really believes life is *routine* in the negative sense. Not always. But, I know there *is* part of him that sees life as one day rolling into the next in order to keep putting food on the table.

My dad taught me something as I watched him through the years, and I don't think he even knows he did. While my dad does have a touch of that working-man, blue-collar, you-work-and-then-you-die perspective, he also is one of the most spontaneous people I know. Sometimes, to a fault. *Like, the time he bought that Triumph TR-7 convertible sports car because our family needed a new car and drove it home with me to show my then-pregnant mom.* On most days, my dad was (and still is) spontaneous in all the good ways. He'd take off a day of work to go boating. He'd stop and buy ice cream. He'd buy the good steak. He'd drive home the long way. He'd stop at the river, and we'd go swimming with our clothes on.

I used to work for my dad (he's a retired painting contractor), and I ran his business for a while as a young man. When I was painting with my dad, I never thought work was routine, even though my dad made those jests. My dad is a comedian when he's at work. He'd make up songs as he painted and dance as he sprayed cabinets. He'd joke with the other subcontractors. He'd give everyone on the job a nickname.

The more I worked for my dad, the more I realized that he found joy in the mundane because he never let it become mundane. He'd always get excited about a new job. He loved it when we branched off into the more artistic side of the business and I did all the faux finishes for the company. He found joy in keeping the paint brushes clean and combing them out at the end of the day because, "They are our livelihood."

When I was nine years old, my parents made a very seemingly spontaneous, risky, fearless, and daring decision to sell everything and try something new. I went with my dad to buy a brand-new, avocado green, Volkswagen Westfalia camper off the lot. He had them install a CB radio and an upgraded stereo system. "Put in the best stereo system you've got," I can still hear my dad say (it was a Blaupunkt, AM/FM stereo, cassette player, with Pioneer speakers, in case you're wondering). My dad then drove me to Tower Records and told me to pick out whatever cassettes I wanted because we were going on a trip. For the next three months, my parents took my brother and I on a trip around the United States looking for a new place to live and a new lifestyle (in case you're wondering, our CB handle was The Green Machine).

My parents model spontaneity in the midst of the mundane. There's an ongoing joke in our family that whenever my dad likes something my mom has made to eat, he says, "Put this one in the book" as if my mom keeps a running cookbook full of dad's favorite recipes. I'd hear this conversation often as I was growing up and my mom would always say, "Okay." There is no book. Truth is, I don't know that my mom ever followed a recipe when she cooked. It was always a reasonable facsimile of the thing she made before.

When you live life without strict guidelines about how to go about your . . . routine, you allow for your routine to become *unusual*. An **unusual routine** is one where there is always an element of surprise in the regular flow of things. These surprises create and condition a mindset for every Idea Mentalist to see things in a new light and never fall prey to the same ol' same ol' mentality.

Truth be told, science tells us that routine without change actually creates ruts in our brains. According to Srini Pillay's article, "Can you rewire your brain to get out of a rut (Yes you can . . .)" from Harvard Health Publishing, the brain creates these ruts due to habitual electrical patterns.

> Faced with new situations, our brains will apply rules based on prior events to match the current context." The part of the brain that does this is called the *dorsolateral prefrontal cortex*. It's what's called the brain's *pattern seeker*. This brain region, it seems, is always working to "circumvent" the "chore" of having to learn something new. On top of all this, some of our routine experiences and relationships that make us feel (or once made us feel) safe, comforted, secure, and at peace with ourselves can lead to, "boredom, depression, unconscious anxiety, or a debilitating addiction. (Pillay 2018)

It seems there is a part of our brain that wants to be lazy. It wants to settle in. It wants the path of least resistance. It *doesn't* want to create new ideas. We definitely need this part of the brain, however. As I understand it, the DLPFC is maturing all your life so, as an adult, you have muscle memory for basic things like cognitive flexibility, working memory, and problem solving.

There is also a part of our brain that *wants* to learn called the *cerebrum*. I like to imagine the *dorsolateral prefrontal cortex* and the *cerebrum* in a war for your ideas (I'm really sure it doesn't work quite like that). But doctors, psychologists, and brain researchers do tell us we can rest the *dorsolateral prefrontal cortex* while other parts of the brain are exercised. Ideas won't come unless we exercise those other parts.

I'm no scientist and maybe I shouldn't have even started down this path of trying to explain the brain. But at a bare minimum I find it interesting and easy to conceive that science confirms there is a war going on inside us to either settle down or press ahead. To rest easy or climb the mountain. To go with the flow or risk change.

We need change. Every one of us. We can let change wash over us and deal with it or we can be part of it. The idea *enthusiast* will never be an Idea Mentalist without embracing change. Change must be a way of life for the Idea Mentalist. Change is the pathway out of the ruts.

Explore Your Town

Speaking of ruts, let's talk about breaking out of them with a *driving* example. What's in your town? Most people have a pretty good idea of what's in their town based on the places they need to get to, e.g., work, school, Target, the grocery store. But, way fewer people know the whole of their town. Few people will drive the side streets, the alleys, the back roads, or the long way home. Fewer people will take a day *just* to explore the town they live in. Even fewer will make it a *habit* to explore their town, know their town, know the sites, know the history, etc.

Quite a few years ago, I delivered furniture for a locally owned store. I knew the name of every street in the town I lived in. I knew the fastest routes. I knew every pit stop along the way. I knew where every corner store resided. I knew where the police cars liked to hang for speed traps.

Before Google Maps, I could draw you an entire map of the town. Eventually, I heard myself describing things to others based on landmarks and house colors—things that other people didn't notice. "It's right past the brown shingle Craftsman home off of Neil Street." "Where's Neil Street?" someone would ask. I was always surprised by questions that seemed obvious to me. It's not like these streets were out in the woods. "What? It's only one street off of Main."

I learned as I was delivering furniture that knowing your town has more benefits than the pride of navigation expertise. I noticed the details of my town that others didn't readily notice. And, noticing details is part of an Idea Mentalist's mentality. Idea Mentalists are constantly increasing the space of their ROM in their mental hard drives.

I'm not a computer geek, but I do know the difference between RAM and ROM (I think. First I try to explain the brain and now computers. I'm really out of my league here). ROM (read-only memory) holds data without power. RAM (random-access memory) is for temporary storage. Be thankful for RAM when you are researching for a paper and have a bunch of apps and windows open at one time and are quickly changing between tasks. When your computer is off, be thankful for ROM since you just typed that huge paper.

When you do things like explore your town, you work to break out of ruts and start to notice new details. Then, you begin storing those details. Your amazing brain keeps storing those details, and one day those details may all add up to present the solution to a problem or a new way of doing things—an idea—a *new* thought introduced to the present situation as a proposal for a course of action (our working definition).

Drive Through New Cities

In much the same way, exploring new cities will expand your mind and help you break out of mind ruts. But, the big difference between exploring your own town and exploring new cities is that new cities often have an entirely different culture than yours and all of a sudden you begin to create new file systems in your ROM.

In new cities, people often talk differently and look different. Oftentimes, restaurant choices are drastically different from your town's. Parks may be bigger or smaller. Transportation choices may vary. Maybe it's a walking city and there's no way you could imagine walking your city. Maybe there's an increase in bike usage. Maybe they have a bike rental system, and your town is just learning about the value of Uber. Maybe the new city has taxis, and you've never taken a ride from a stranger.

New cities are full of sensory input that is unique to the region and culture. New cities force us to try new things. New cities can be like visiting a new country.

I know a woman who lives three hours from Chicago. She's lived her entire life in a small town in Michigan where people go to sheep-shearing events and maple syrup festivals. Her town has an annual hot air balloon festival, and she lives just a few miles from the Michigan Speedway. She regularly hosts backyard bonfires and family potlucks. When her town got their first Starbucks, you'd think someone had invented the wheel. Some people loved it and saw it as a sign of progress, others believed it was a sign of the Apocalypse. The *first time* my friend visited Chicago, she was in her fifties It took her fifty-plus years to visit one of the greatest cities in the world, only three hours from her!

I know a man who grew up in Chicago. He also spent some time in Detroit. Two big and influential cities (though Chicago is much bigger). He spent most of his days going to professional baseball games, golfing with clients, walking throughout the city, eating at different restaurants, never cooking at home, going to plays and musicals, and running the finances of a huge company. He moved to my other friend's Michigan town a few years ago (the woman and town from the story above).

To talk to each of them about their different city experiences is a mind job. For my small-town friend, Chicago was confusing, snooty, disorienting, expensive, fast-paced, overrated, overpopulated, smelly, and exhausting. For my Chicago-born friend, his new town doesn't provide many choices for entertainment or dining, is boring, uneventful, hard to get around, backwoods and simple, slow, uncultured, and not very smart.

The fact is, they both need a little of the other to expand their thinking. They both need a saturated experience to embrace everything the other culture has to offer them to make them better and more well-rounded human beings. They both have attitudes that are unhealthy. They both have created ruts in their thinking about the way life "should" be. And, neither of them will be the kind of Idea Mentalist they *could* be until they learn what life *could* be in the other culture *if they fully embraced it.*

Each of their cultures surface different problems and provide different solutions. Each of their cultures has needs the other culture might have an answer for. Each of their cultures has stories and people that make up the uniqueness and recipe for what makes them each so special. Each of them has experiences the other culture couldn't recreate even if it wanted to.

Take Other Routes

I drive my family crazy. Rather, my family goes crazy when I'm driving. Or both.

The following is a fictitious conversation . . . that happens all the time. "You missed the turn!" No, I didn't. I'm going a new way. "But this way is longer!" The response in my brain is, "Yes, it is. Or, maybe it isn't, but you wouldn't know because you aren't used to going this way and have never tried it. Just let me drive."

I like to take the *other way* home. The long way home. The different way home. It's along these routes that I see new things, meet new people, experience how other people live, see what homes are for sale, see what homes are being built, see what new businesses are starting, see what businesses have gone under, see new views of my town, and . . . take a load off. Taking other routes is a good way to expose yourself to new stimuli and it's also a good way to just unwind and free your creative mind space of the things you've been renting the space out to.

In the book *Flex: Do Something Different*, Ben Fletcher and Karen Pine suggest there are enormous costs to us being too habitual. They conclude the brain is hard-wired to operate on what they call the "efficiency principle" to keep it from having to work overtime to figure out small problems. This rings true with the *dorsolateral prefrontal cortex* concept we learned earlier. Our brains naturally want us to stop over-thinking. While efficiency and conserving our brain's resources sound like a good idea at first glance, Fletcher and Pine say, ". . . this efficiency principle has a cost."

> Automatacity—being at the mercy of our narrow personality—means there will be new experiences that we try to solve with old models. Our constantly changing life will present us with opportunities that we will fail to notice . . . Unless we can flex, we will fail to act upon life as it is in this very moment. (223)

The authors suggest that tiny things like changing your route to work or home begins to train your mind to think differently and not react on autopilot. Theoretically speaking, these tiny changes and flexibility can lead to a chain of actions and reactions. Or, at least, they begin to condition us and put us in a better place to be able to seize new opportunities and be willing to embrace change—which, for the Idea Mentalist, is an exciting notion.

I know from personal experience that the more you break from the norm and take other routes, the more you will notice change along your more regularly traveled route. I mentioned earlier I sometimes let my dogs lead the way on morning walks. They like taking new routes and marking new trails as their territory. Recently, I decided to make the decision for them and go on a walk on a path I used to frequent. It had only been about twelve weeks since we took this particular path, and I couldn't believe the change. A home had been built on an empty lot, a store had gone out of business, another home had been painted, a front yard had been landscaped, a new restaurant building that had barely broken ground three months earlier was getting the final touches on its exterior, and a part of the sidewalk that had been closed had reopened after work crews widened the road.

There were other kinds of revelations when I went back to the old path—I was surprised at how much *hadn't* changed. That pile of garbage was still in that front yard. That house was still for sale. That 1968 VW Bug hadn't moved an inch. That bike was still chained to a pole.

Changing our route helps us experience new things, and it gives us a fresh perspective on the old route when we return to it. We see the things that have changed, and we see the things that should have changed. At the very least, we might question why they are the same.

I believe there is both a mental and a metaphorical connection between changing our route and changing our routine.

By the way, route and routine come from the same French word. The words have nuances of something habitual. Just as changing your habitual course of travel can help you see new things, changing your habitual course of work, play, study, relationships, entertainment, food choices, etc., can also help you see new things.

On the path to becoming an Idea Mentalist, changing your route is important in learning how to change your routine. If you can create new habits in the way you travel, I believe it will help you create new habits in the way you work, think, and dream.

Eat *Somewhere* Else. Eat *Something* Else.

In the beginning of this book, I said, "My favorite restaurant is the one I haven't been to yet." That's mostly true. I do have some favorites I like to return to, but, for the most part, I like to experience new dining environments. When I'm craving that special something, of course I'm going to go to my favorite restaurants to satisfy that craving. But, I refuse to let myself become a restaurant creature of habit. When it comes to restaurants, the Idea Mentalist's habit should be *to not have a habit*.

Idea Mentalists must embrace change. Sometimes on the path to becoming an Idea Mentalist, you will need to train yourself to acquire *new tastes* in order to embrace change. A good training ground is restaurant and food choice.

When I lived in the Midwest, our town didn't have many restaurant choices. We had even fewer good ones. There was a total of about four decent restaurants to choose from in our struggling town. Try as I might to visit new restaurants all the time with clients, I would end up circling back around to the beginning sooner or later. But, what I *could* do was change up my choices on the menu. I made it a game to try new things on the menus of our limited dining establishments. I wanted to be able to answer questions about anything on the menu if I was ever with a client. *"Have you tried the tomato soup?"* Yes. I have. They make it from scratch. However, it has more garlic than you might expect. *"Have you tried the brisket?"* You bet. It melts in your mouth.

By the way, did you know the older you get, the less taste buds you have? You also produce less saliva the older you get, which limits your ability to taste. Because your sense of taste works in connection with your sense of smell and your ability to smell can also diminish with age, your sense of taste is even more at risk. Your ability to enjoy different flavors and appreciate new foods is a precious commodity that should be cherished and enjoyed. Science also tells us that eating the same foods over and over reduces our ability to distinguish taste. This shouldn't be surprising since we've already discussed how our mind wants to work on autopilot.

When I moved back to California from the Midwest, there were so many restaurant choices that my wife and I made it a game to not visit the same restaurant twice for an entire year. At the same time, I ran a Monday morning meeting at work that I decided to host at local coffee shops and, for the first year, we didn't go to the same spot twice.

For three years, my wife and I went to a different coffee shop every Friday. This isn't always an option for everyone, but I highly recommend it. We set our radius at one hour from home when we were picking places to go, which expanded our horizons. The Idea Mentalist will begin to take note of all the subtle restaurant differences and the things that make each experience unique. All the while, you'll be expanding your ROM. Each experience has new people, aesthetics, systems, smells, tastes, furniture, and personality.

I mentioned I don't eat or drink at chains. I stick to locally owned, locally resourced, locally managed, locally designed stores as much as possible. There's the occasional carpool ride where someone wants to eat or drink at a chain, but I avoid them whenever possible. Besides the economic and ethical convictions I have about buying local, I believe the local shop will offer you that special something that no one else offers. They are the boutiques and laboratories of your town. They must be innovative. They must change. These are the kinds of establishments the Idea Mentalist wants to frequent and pay attention to.

Play a Different Instrument

I don't know if you are a musician like me. If you aren't, you can still dial in to what I'm about to say and use it as a guiding metaphor. You will be able to apply this concept to any number of things including software, environment, food, craft, and tools.

I play guitar. Predominantly. I play a few other instruments, but not nearly as well. My second instrument would probably be piano.

I've written quite a few songs over the years. I get to perform my music in local environments often—bars, coffee shops, theaters, pubs, wine bars. I love telling stories with a guitar in my hand.

For some reason, for most of my life I wrote songs from the guitar, even though I play other instruments. I don't know if it was my lack of confidence, habit, or the fact that I can't really carry a piano with me to gigs that kept me writing from guitar.

I remember one significant day in my life where I didn't have my guitar with me, but I had a song idea. A piano was the only thing within reach. The piano had been sitting in my home for years, but I rarely sat at it. My kids and my wife made more use of it.

Stuck with my secondary instrument, I began writing a song. As I played, I realized I arpeggiated my chords differently because of the layout of the piano. I also began playing chords that weren't the usual go-to chords for me on the guitar. I also played piano with a less percussive attack than I did with guitar. Because of the sustain on the piano, my chords were allowed to hang in the air longer and individual notes filled the space differently. What began flowing from my fingers was a totally different song than I had imagined.

I started crying.

As I wrote lyrics, the timbre of the piano seemed to influence, inform, and maybe even dictate my poetry. The structure of the song was different from anything I had ever written. When I played the song for my friend, he asked, "Who wrote that?"

Truth is, I never would have written the song if I had a guitar in my hand. Not that song. Not those lyrics. Not that feel. Not that emotion.

The Idea Mentalist can be in an idea rut without even knowing it. While I was in the habit of writing new songs from the guitar, I was also cementing a rubric of sorts the more I stayed with guitar as my primary writing instrument. The piano unveiled a new part of my soul where other songs were held captive by my routine.

If you handcraft toys, lay down the power tools and take a trip to a thrift store to invest in some old hand tools. If you are a chef, try buying ingredients you never use and begin to experiment. If you build spec homes, quit painting your walls beige and take a trip to the paint store for a color deck. If you throw dinner parties in your backyard, imagine what one could look like in your front yard.

Dress Differently

One of my favorite activities to do with groups is to take them hat shopping at a really expressive and diverse hat shop. There's a little game I've played with teams over the years where I instruct the team to try on a few different hats that are in their comfort zone and take selfies wearing the hats they choose. Then, they must also allow the other team members to dress them in hats that the *team* thinks they would look good in. More selfies. It's always an amazing thing to see baseball-hat-guy wearing a cowboy hat. It's fun to see bandana-lady wearing a steampunk top hat.

We often don't try on other hats because we aren't *comfortable* in them. Or, we don't think we can pull them off. Or, we've just never thought about it. It's always rewarding to be with a team that compliments you and cheers you on for wearing a hat you never imagined putting on your noggin.

Many times, team members leave the store with a new hat. And a new posture. And a new attitude.

Sidenote: 99% of the people I've done the above exercise with end up having a great time. Once I did it with a group and two people complained I wasted their time. Some people won't get it when you do things differently. Some people don't understand how things can be fun and productive at the same time. Some people reserve the right to be a boring, never-changing, complaining, cotton-headed-ninny-muggins. Just move on.

Look at performers like Lady Gaga, Madonna, Lenny Kravitz, The Beatles, David Bowie, and Prince. Each of them drastically changed (or keeps changing) their look with almost every album. You don't have to be an audiophile to to hear how their sound changes with their aesthetic. And each time they change, they own a little more of the music world.

For ten seasons, running from 2003 to 2013, the TLC network aired the show *What Not to Wear*. On the show, fashionistas Stacy London and Clinton Kelly would surprise a "style felon" nominated by their friends or family to receive a style makeover with the prerequisite of tossing out their old clothing and going on a $5,000 shopping spree. While many of the contestants were just stuck in a fashion time-warp, some wore their clothing as some sort of metaphor for their soul that had decided to give up on life. For those who had truly become downcast people, the ambush by London and Kelly played very much like an intervention for an addict.

The *reveal* at the end was always the best part of the show—when men and women were finally able to bare their new, confident self to their friends, families, and coworkers after weeks of grueling, often painful, teasing criticism of their unflattering and flawed taste in clothing. While I didn't approve of the mocking that contestants had to endure, I was always happy for them in the end. It takes guts to toss a closet full of things that have become a comfort to you. However, sometimes it's this kind of cataclysmic change we need to begin to think differently. As the credits rolled, contestants would be seen modeling other items in their new wardrobe and talking about how the experience had changed them, gave them confidence, and got them out of a rut.

Clothing can be a rut. The more ruts we stay in, the more our brains rest. The creative energy becomes a little more atrophied. Idea Mentalists realize that even something as simple as fabric can keep us from thinking in new ways. The reason people seldom change their wardrobe is *fear.* Fear is a poison and poison has no place in the apothecary of an Idea Mentalist.

Once upon a time, as a young father, I tried doing life in Dockers and golf shirts. That may be your style (and I'm not knocking it) but *this guy* was not made for that wardrobe. I'm more vintage thrift than J.Crew. More Levi's than PacSun. More Harley than golf cart. More t-shirt than collar. More hippie than preppie. But, the job I had at the time had me doing life in a culture and living in a town with people who dressed much differently than I wanted to. I was a punk-rock artist in a computer-industry town. Still, I conformed. I gravitated to the lowest common denominator of their apparel and became a clone. We were one, happy, uniform community.

And I was miserable.

And I had no energy.

And I was depressed.

My friend Patrick is a rock star. Literally and figuratively. He came for a visit after not seeing me for a couple of years, witnessed my despondency, and asked if he could help. I thought we were going for a drink, but instead, he took me shopping.

That trip to the store(s) changed my life that day. Somewhere along the line, I allowed myself to buy a lie that I had to wear a certain wardrobe to be accepted in my community, respected for my ideas, and trusted. After I changed my wardrobe, I found exactly the opposite was true. People complimented me on my shirts and said things like, "I wish I had the guts to wear that." People commented on my huge sunglasses and said, "I wish I could pull those off." My confidence level shot through the roof with my new-found freedom of wardrobe expression.

Soon after my wardrobe change, I changed my job. We moved to another state. We started new business ventures. Call me crazy, but I credit Patrick and throwing out my old closet with the boost to my self-confidence that helped change the trajectory of my life. The clearance rack has become a metaphor for daring change for me. Often, the shirts that are too bright, too edgy, too artsy, or too quirky end up on the rack because no one else wanted them. It's then that I sweep in for the goods.

Imagine expanding your wardrobe and being confident with so many different styles that you could feel confident in a variety of situations—some where few people dare to go. Imagine being able to morph into any dinner party scenario without wondering, "Do I look okay in this?" Imagine expanding your clothing and accessory palate where you never feel awkward in a costume. That may feel like a tall order for you, but at least you can start with a new pair of shoes. Or a new dress. Or pants without pleats.

I have a hat rack in my room with no less than twenty hats on it. Because I can. *"Who says I can't wear that?"*

Go to a Different Movie

In literature, a *trope* is non-conventional language, phrases, images, or poetic devices used for artistic and dramatic effect. "Trope" can also refer to familiar images, music, themes, templates, and clichés in the movies or other creative works. My wife likes to watch Hallmark movies and I like to tease her for watching them—because of the tropes. You'll never get surprised by the twist in a Hallmark movie.

1. Girl meets guy.
2. She is not impressed.
3. Something brings them together.
4. She is surprised they fall in love.
5. We are not surprised by anything.

My favorite tropes are in horror and thriller movies. In a horror movie, if someone goes to the bathroom wall-mounted medicine cabinet, grabs the corners of the sink, stares for a few seconds at themselves, splashes water on their face, then opens the medicine cabinet, get ready for a huge surprise when that mirrored door shuts. Nearly 100% of the time, someone will be behind them with a grotesque face, axe in their head, or holding a knife. Cue scream. We're so used to this that we anticipate the surprise and are shocked when it doesn't happen. Which is a surprise in and of itself. Beware the second shutting of the medicine cabinet.

If running from a monster or murderer, a character will most likely run into the woods, trip over something, hurt themselves, and hide very poorly as the killer breathes on their neck. If kids are in the woods with a flashlight, it will most likely go out. If J.J. Abrams has anything to do with what you are watching, there will be some kind of tunnel or abandoned building with flickering lights inside. The electricity is always on and there's always a bad connection in scary places.

It's interesting that the word trope has etymologized to mean something that becomes commonplace and expected. Trope comes from the Greek verb, *trepein,* that means, "to turn, to direct, to alter, to change." Tropes are meant to bring about a change in the story—the element of surprise, the instilling of fear, the surprise twist that alters your predictions. It's ironic that the trope is what we now expect.

My friend plays a game where he goes to the theater whenever he wants and buys a ticket to whatever is playing next. He seldom picks a movie because everyone else is seeing it. He loves the element of surprise. And, he loves getting exposed to things outside of his own particular taste in story. He will never be guilty of always gravitating to specific tropes.

In the spirit of expanding our palates, not falling into ruts, not becoming predictable to those around us, conditioning ourselves to embrace change, and training our brains to think differently, the Idea Mentalist must embrace new stories and genres.

Read a Different Book

For all the same reasons the Idea Mentalist should go to a different movie, they should read outside their habitual genres and field of interest. Reading different books can also provide a new level of interaction and stretching for the brain when we take our book suggestions from someone who is passionate about the book they are suggesting.

Book club formats where individuals take turns picking the group reading can be a helpful kick in the pants for reading new material we wouldn't normally pick out—that is, if the group is diverse enough in their tastes.

Years ago, I worked with another individual who was in leadership with me. We never read the same things. If I was reading fiction, he was reading business books. If I was reading books about change and innovation, he was reading about management styles. We found we were often at odds with one another in meetings—partly due to the fact that we were being informed by what we were reading.

We started a habit of taking turns picking books to read together. While we still disagreed on many levels, our disagreements became much more civil and filled with mutual understanding. We both began to think differently. There were even a couple of times where I found myself quoting an author he had suggested and vice versa.

Vacation Somewhere Different

Painting with large brushstrokes, I believe one of the worst vacation decisions one can make is to invest in a timeshare. I do have a friend that would disagree. He's a world traveler as part of his job and his timeshare (that they use often) is an oasis for them—a place they look forward to. A place they use often. A place they rent out to others. One time, he took us to his timeshare, and I am *so* grateful he has it.

But, he's an anomaly.

Besides the usually horrible financial repercussions of timeshare investment, it's the part about being *stuck* that should give the Idea Mentalist the chills. *Many* more of my friends have timeshare stories where they get bored of the place they invested in, seldom go, always feel guilty about throwing their money away when it goes unused, and they end up spending more money on vacation than they had ever planned because their timeshare is in mid-Michigan, but they'd rather go on a cruise. So, they do.

My wife and I make vacations a habit. We work hard and we play hard. We go wherever we want as long as we've saved the money to pay cash for the trip. I do side gigs like playing music, consulting, and speaking, and we save that money in an account we refer to as our "Marriage Insurance" account.

My wife loves planning our vacations. We often try to experience a new National Park because we are trying to see all of them before we die. We also take in a myriad of experiences along the way to the parks. One of my favorite things to do is to allow my wife to pick all our ancillary experiences as well as our route. Of course, from time to time I pick something I want to experience in the area we are visiting, but my wife is an insane researcher with an intuition for new experiences we'd enjoy. New restaurants. National landmarks. Roadside curiosities. She plans them out months in advance. She makes multiple reservations. And I get in the truck, Airstream behind us, and ask, "Where are we going today?"

The Idea Mentalist must become comfortable with someone else planning experiences for them occasionally. The truth is, no one is ever truly in control of their entire life, and people make decisions for us all the time. Allowing someone else to plan the occasional experience or vacation for us forces the Idea Mentalist to approach every experience with an inquisitive perspective—ready and willing to learn new things.

There is often comfort in returning to the same places we like to visit. The family mountain cabin. That little Airbnb cabana by the water. Disneyland. Sometimes reliving memories is the perfect elixir to our soul. But, Idea Mentalists should be aware and beware. The more routine habits we create in our lives, the more we create potential to become less accepting of embracing change and new ideas.

Order Magazines You've Never Ordered

Under normal circumstances and being of sound mind, I would never choose to buy nine ounces of popcorn for $18. Who would? You'd have to be starving with $18 to your name in a desert where popcorn is your only option for survival. But, school fundraisers have weaseled $18 out of me on more than one occasion for this exact item.

School fundraisers are successful by capitalizing on guilt and adults being manipulated by children with cute smiles and hopes of prizes and accolades. I usually cringe at the fundraiser knock on my front door or the candy bar box sitting with a signup list on the counter at work. I feel like if my name is not on the list of orders, I'll look like a jerk who doesn't care about children. If I send the cute kid off my porch without a sale, my neighbors will probably find out about it and judge me. Of course, I must buy them from my grandchildren no matter what.

Knowing I am going to be suckered into buying *something* throughout the school year, I used to hope my kids would do magazine sale fundraisers for their schools instead of sweets. Magazines don't put my A1C (average blood glucose) at risk. I can learn from magazines. I can expand my thinking with magazines.

Next time you are encouraged (forced) to buy magazines for a fundraiser, I dare you to order something you would never pick up off the shelf at Walgreens. Magazines are designed to play to a specific demographic—that's how they work. Motorcycle enthusiasts buy motorcycle magazines. Fashionistas by fashion magazines. But, imagine what would happen if a motorcycle enthusiast bought a fashion magazine. They'd see a whole new world. They'd learn of new products. Maybe new places. Maybe they'd learn something about someone they work with. Maybe they'd think differently about their own appearance.

Idea Mentalists are always learning new things about the world around them and the people they do life with. This requires stretching and investing in worlds we aren't used to, don't understand, and sometimes aren't aware even exist.

Collect Something . . . Different

Years ago, I started collecting tobacco pipes. When I started, I knew nothing about pipes. My grandfather willed me his tool collection when he passed, and his pipe was in the top drawer of a toolbox he gave me. I filled it with tobacco one day, took a puff, thought about Grandpa, and decided I would start collecting pipes.

Collecting pipes has been an aesthetic adventure. They look cool. There are multiple styles and shapes—the Acorn, the Apple, the Billiard, the Calabash, the Tankard, the Churchwarden, the list goes on. There are travel pipes, short-stemmed, long-stemmed, free-standing, solid, two-piece, and we're just getting started. There are pipes made of corncob, briar, meerschaum, glass, high-tech carbon, bone, soapstone, and a variety of other materials.

But, the greatest thing about collecting pipes for me is in the acquisition of the pipes. I collect pipes from places I visit. I collect from estate sales. Sometimes, friends buy me pipes. All my pipes have stories. I'm not in the business of simply buying pipes online from some mass production house or cheap retailer.

My pipe collection has put me in touch with hundreds of people I wouldn't have otherwise met. I've had countless conversations with strangers about pipes. I've been invited to see other pipe collections because of my interest. I've been to small tobacconist shops where I've sat for hours hearing stories from people thirty years my senior.

The Idea Mentalist is always looking for ways to meet new people and experience new passions. They are always going out of their way to find special gems. Quite frankly, out-of-their-way is their *only* way.

Rent a Vehicle and Dream Drive

One of my favorite things to do is rent a vehicle. I love picking rides that I will probably never own or never drive unless I rent it. This doesn't mean I only rent expensive cars or sports cars. I want to experience something new, and a different car provides a different experience.

It's always interesting to me to see if a vehicle is user-friendly. Can I find the defrost easy enough? Is it easy to locate the hazard lights? Can I operate the radio without driving off the road? Different accessory configurations keep me on my toes.

I like to ask the vehicle what kind of music it likes to listen to, as if it has a soul. Some cars require rock and roll. Others like to be mellow. Others require me to listen to music genres I usually don't listen to.

Once I figure out how to correctly operate the functions I need to utilize, and once I allow the car to pick the music, I love hitting the road. It's on the road that I dream.

When I dream, I ask questions about what kind of person would typically drive the car I'm driving. What is their line of work? What places do they frequent? What is their name? What do they think about when they're listening to Eminem in this Mustang? What is going through their mind as they listen to Train in this minivan? Where would they stop for lunch as they listen to Lady Gaga in this SUV? I try to put myself into the mindset of the blue-collar worker, the soccer mom, the cowboy, the rocker, or whomever might be driving the vehicle I drive.

What is this vehicle telling me? What is this music telling me? What is this restaurant I stopped at for lunch telling me? They are all telling us something. If we listen.

Sounds like a game, right? It is. The Idea Mentalist is always creating games out of life as they try on new experiences. Games make life more enjoyable. When we enjoy life, there is less space in our brain for worry, fear, and dismay. That leaves more space in our brain for creativity, abundant life, and new ideas.

Shop Other Stores

By now, you should have a clear idea of what I mean when I say, "Everything New." This chapter has provided you with quite a few ideas of how you can un-organize, mess up, and un-predict your routine and get your mind out of a rut so it can think differently. However, at the risk of sounding redundant, I'll give us one more thing to try on for size.

I mentioned earlier it's my goal to know every shop owner and employee in every store in my town. The reason I want to do that is because they are my people. They make up my town and I want to know them. But, I also want to know their stores. Stores have a personality.

There is a western-wear store in my town that has been there since 1961. Family-owned. It looks and smells different than any clothing store in town. It is a boutique of sorts. They advertise differently than the chain stores. The music is different. And, the employees are over-the-top helpful and courteous. In some ways, I feel like I step back into 1961 when I enter the store. In all the good ways.

Stores bring in different personalities. If I always shop at Target, I will always run into the same Target people. If I always shop at Hot Topic, I will see the same Hot Topic patrons. Not to mention, these stores have a style, and if I always buy my clothes there, I will look like them. This is reason enough to not get stuck shopping in one store.

Beyond not getting stuck, new experiences often lead to new ideas. At the very least, experiencing new things will help you think differently and not be conditioned by familiar surroundings.

Experiencing new things is not always a direct connect-the-dots to a new idea. However, every once in a while, a walk into a new store will prompt an on-the-spot idea.

I used to take a team of people to Chicago every year to participate in an event I called *24²*. This event was invitation-only and was only for people who were serious about becoming Idea Mentalists. The rules are simple: Find twenty-four inspiring ideas in twenty-four hours and document them with photographs. Maybe it's an aesthetic that catches the eye, maybe a service-oriented idea, maybe a new tactile experience like a new food prepared in a unique way.

This 24^2 event often spawned transferable ideas or rhyming ideas for the participant's organizations. In Chapter One, we defined an idea as "a *new* thought introduced to the present situation as a proposal for a course of action." Exercises like a 24^2 event can often stimulate new thoughts for one's current situation based on something they saw in another application.

One year, when Joe saw the display for the (RED) iPhone campaign in Chicago, something clicked for him. The sleek counter, matching shirts, and technology made him think about his big company back home and how people were always complaining that it was hard to be "in the know" at their huge campus. Joe left that 24^2 event and started a "bar" much like the Apple Genius Bar at his company. The slick new information center boasted friendly people who were easy to find if you had a question. As a bonus, Joe and his team worked to put together an audio tour of their campus, and folks were able to check out headphones at their new bar for a tour that walked guests through frequently asked questions.

A light went on in Meg when she walked around taking photos in Chicago. One store she walked into had a photo display of people and places around Chicago. In that instant, a new idea was born for her. Her little Midwest town had developed a bit of the *poor me's* and she now had an idea to breathe life into her town. She returned home and hosted a photo contest for her town. The collection of photos that included abandoned and dilapidated buildings as well as parks and flowers became a book complete with poems and sayings about hope. Hundreds of copies were sold in her town and the money was donated to charity.

So, yes. Sometimes a new experience, like shopping in a new store, can produce immediate results for the Idea Mentalist if he or she is paying attention and thinking proactively. Walking into a new store and asking questions like, "What can I learn here?" and, "How is this store like life?" can produce surprising results.

Everything New Might Suck

You might be a creature of habit and new things are a huge stretch for you. Don't give up.

You might create a little anxiety for yourself as you shed your old skin. Don't give up.

You might try "Everything New" for a while, not get immediate results, and be tempted to think, "Eh, that's good enough." Don't give up.

Years ago, I learned my blood sugar was higher than it should be. I didn't want to go on medication, so I started reading about how I could control diabetes. My mother-in-law turned me on to a book called *The Fast Metabolism Diet* that changed my world. Since I started eating the "Fast Metabolism" way, I've lost a good amount of weight and my sugars are in check. I didn't think I ate unhealthily before I started this new way of eating, but the plan was definitely a new way of eating for me.

In a nutshell, I now eat certain foods on certain days and avoid certain foods on certain days, which allows my body to fuel some internal systems while others are resting and vice versa. I eat every two to three hours. I drink a ton of water. I do aerobic exercise on Mondays and Tuesdays. Wednesday and Thursdays are weight training days. Fridays through Sundays are casual and full of things that give me life like walks, spending time with grandkids, playing music, and writing.

New habits, new experiences, and new perspectives are often like healthy diets. Starting them can suck.

When I started eating healthy, it was difficult. I had never eaten so many vegetables and fruit in my life. I wasn't used to denying myself certain foods on certain days. Drinking half my body weight in ounces of water was no fun at first and I peed every twenty minutes. I cut regular dairy consumption out of my diet because I learned it's not really good for us and I'm allergic to it. Before eating healthy, I ate cheese all the time and dealt with the consequences. Stopping was hard.

After a while, something strange happened. I started craving all the things that were hard for me to embrace. Now, I can't imagine eating differently. I'm healthier, happier, and less stressed. As I type this, I'm craving some celery and homemade cashew butter

Here's another strange thing . . . food tastes different to me now.

I started using different spices, hot sauces, coconut aminos. I started cooking occasionally with coconut oil. I introduced new vegetables. I developed new recipes.

For a man who never ate breakfast, never did I think I would wake up craving kale and onions sautéed with sweet potato cubes, avocado spread on sprouted grain toast, and fresh fruit. But, I do. Often.

I enjoy exercise and I never used to. I especially like aerobic activity that allows me to wear headphones and listen to new music, audio books, and podcasts from some wise people while working out. I've learned so much.

So let's get this straight. By trying new things that I hated at first and sticking with it, I am now many pounds lighter, my sugars are in check, I breathe easier, my mind is clearer, and I've been exposed to even more new music, books, and teachers than ever before.

You better believe those new experiences have made me a sharper Idea Mentalist. The new energy I have to experience other things is worth the price of admission.

CHAPTER SIX
GIVE ME MY SPACE

In Chapter Three, we began to touch on the importance of *space* as part of incubating ideas.

But, let's dig a little deeper.

Understanding Proxemics

Proxemics is the study of space and the use of space. The term was used first in the early 1960s by Edward T. Hall—a cultural anthropologist. His work is helpful in understanding how *interpersonal communication* is affected by the spaces we live and work and play in. According to Hall and many who followed in his footsteps, **Public Space, Social Space, Personal Space,** and **Intimate Space** all have rules, boundaries, expectations, and definitions that affect the way we interact with one another.

We carry different expectations into the spaces. For example, Intimate Space is reserved for whispering, touching, hugging, kissing, and sex. But, we don't have those same expectations for Public Space (unless you are part of some weird commune or cult somewhere). Public Space might be a convention, a church service, or a sporting event, and we don't have the same physical contact or needs met in that space. If Edward T. Hall were alive today, I imagine he would now include Cyberspace as a fifth component of human interaction. Though, that's more difficult to define. In my book, *Follow You Follow Me,* I describe this space as the "Not-So Space"—a playful word to say that we are still defining and understanding the boundaries and expectations of the Internet.

The study of proxemics has implications outside of interpersonal communication, such as how physical spaces are arranged and how that affects our ability to connect with the space itself. The Chinese concept of *feng shui* claims that space contains good or bad energy based on how it's arranged and oriented.

The bottom line is that anthropologists, sociologists, and scientists all agree that we are affected by space. Proxemics is a fascinating study (I love it), but even if you aren't familiar with the theories, you intuitively know that space affects you. You also know when something doesn't feel right for the space you're in. You know how it feels when someone invades your space. You may just not stop to think about it.

Did you ever do something naughty as a kid and have to stand in the corner?

Have you ever walked into a very large room or onto a football field all by yourself?

Have you ever been in a crowded elevator?

Have you ever had a stranger strike up a conversation with you in the restroom?

Have you ever seen someone go streaking down the street?

Have you ever had a stranger touch you on the shoulder for an uncomfortable amount of time while standing close to you and talking?

It's way easier to define general social norms and expectations for spaces than it is to define the kind of space that may be helpful for *you* to thrive in. We can describe when someone is *invading our space* and the majority of humans will agree on those rules.

However, curating the space that will work for *you* is partly subjective. Sure, there are some studies that provide some helpful and generic information to help us create good spaces (clear the clutter, have good lighting, organize), but only *you* know what environment will help *you* think better, dream better, imagine better, innovate better, create better, and ideate better. You have your own personality, your own quirks, your own style, your own pet peeves, your own square footage requirements, and your own expectations for any space you occupy. If you don't live and work in ideal spaces now, it's time to make some changes.

For the Idea Mentalist, space matters. Your home. Your place of work. Your creative space. Places you stay on road trips. Spaces can help us or hinder us in our constant quest to become Idea Mentalists. You may not know what you need at this point, which will require some experimentation. When you get there, you will know it.

The first album I ever recorded was done in Vancouver, Washington, and Portland, Oregon. When I hear the songs on the album, all these years later, it's impossible for me to not hear and see the spaces in my mind. I smell the rain, I know the color of the sky, I am reacquainted with the friends I brought into the studio with me and the friends I met during the project.

This is true for every album I've recorded since. Every song I've ever recorded would sound different to the world if it had been recorded in a different space. Musicians know this and often seek out studios and recording spaces that have a special magic. Spaces influence a musician's mood, energy, outlook, attention to detail, and oftentimes the actual songwriting, production, and arrangement of music. In the same way that a musician will write a different piece of music if they write it from a different instrument, their song will be influenced by space. You can put the exact same equipment into two different studios and follow the same exact steps and it will *sound* different. Space influences every part of music.

If you are planning a wedding, your venue will determine much of your aesthetic. If you have an aesthetic in mind, you will choose your venue to match the moment you're trying to create. Barn weddings are a popular venue in the Midwest. I've been to plenty of weddings in barns and they're usually full of line dancing, cowboy hats, moonshine, mason jars, hootin' and hollerin', and bistro lights.

Now imagine having a wedding in an old Catholic church. What does the aesthetic look like? Probably not moonshine and cowboy hats. Is there a mood difference between the venues? Are there different expectations? Of course there are. The people in the old Catholic church wedding go to *another space* to get drunk after. (Hee hee. My little joke.)

Think about your place of work. What does it look like? What are the colors? How is it arranged? How do people dress there? What does it smell like? Is it cluttery? Corporate? Casual? All of these answers influence how people act and think at your place of work. And, if you want to be an Idea Mentalist, it's important to realize just how much space affects your ability to think differently.

I was hired by an organization in Northern California a few years back that felt "stuck." When I got the initial phone call asking if I'd be interested in taking a position, they said, "We need new energy. We need new creativity. We need new ideas." Those things got me very excited. But, I have learned over the years that liking the notion of change and actually possessing a willingness to change are two different things.

Before I said "yes" to the job, I went on a space recon mission. Their space was very corporate. The colors were dated. The walls were mostly blank with an occasional landscape print in a simple frame. Outdated cubicles faced mostly outward and 90% of the people in those cubicles looked at a blank wall. The entry space to the office had exposed mailboxes full of junk sitting behind the receptionist. Random knick-knacks (or, as my wife calls them, *shit-knacks*) filled spaces above cupboards and the tops of metal file cabinets. Dusty, fake plants were in random spots throughout the room as if someone had stuck them there to try and figure out what else to do. There was no space for the entire team to gather.

Knowing how much space and environments influence or inhibit change, I made a long list of observations about their workspace. When I interviewed for the position, I shared a list of possibilities for change based on things that my fresh eyes observed. My list had these words at the top of the page, "What If I . . ." followed by a list of things I would suggest to change. I knew I would not take the job if I kept getting pushback on the suggested changes. Space is that important. If they weren't willing to change their space, they were lying to themselves about new energy, creativity, and ideas.

Here are some of the questions I asked in regard to space:

What if I . . .

   . . . *invest money in art? Real art. Not the kind you buy in the bins at Michaels.*
   . . . *repaint everything. Maybe multiple times?*
   . . . *tear out some office walls?*
   . . . *create a common area for the whole office to enjoy?*
   . . . *move senior leaders out of their offices?*
   . . .*sell your current property?*

Selling the property was the only thing I got pushback on, and I was kinda joking anyway. Kinda. The building structure itself was not and is not conducive to energy, creativity, and ideas. It was built with a function-over-form mentality that many corporations fall prey to and wallow in as they try to retro-fit creativity and beauty. Word to the wise . . . if you are building a place of creativity, don't model it after Costco. If you do, and you desire change, you'll always fight against that space.

Within three years, the space was completely transformed. New paint colors. New art by local artists. Mailboxes relocated. A more inviting receptionist area. The biggest space improvement of all was the creation of a common area for the staff to imagine and innovate, laugh, and strategize.

If you ask the staff what happened to their energy, creativity, and ideas over that three-year period of time, you will hear amazing stories on personal and corporate levels. People who didn't think they were that creative began bringing ideas to the table and following through with new direction for the company. Space wasn't the only thing that initiated those changes, but it was a huge component. Space doesn't create ideas, but it certainly can create an environment ripe for ideas.

Side note: You won't hear stories of growth from the people who didn't like the changes and left the company, in part, because of the changes. Some people reserve the right to hate change. Some people hated me for making change. Such is life.

Side note two: The space I reimagined still has much room for improvement and sometime soon the space will need to change again. Or, everyone will experience Space Atrophy once again.

Side note three: This same company fired me in large part due to my ideas. It was super painful when it happened. I'm thrilled I am no longer there. It is a huge drag to be on a team with people that fear change. More on this later.

Space Atrophy a.k.a. Dead Space

We talk about *atrophy* in a number of ways. The most common way is when we talk about body tissue and organs. If we don't exercise our muscles, they begin to atrophy. Degenerate. Get weak. They no longer work. We also talk about atrophy when we are describing skill sets. If a dancer stops dancing, eventually their skills will not be sharp. They won't have the same muscle memory. Their body won't do the same things it used to do when they were at the height of their game. Their dance skills will *atrophy*. The same rules apply for artists, engineers, technicians, physicians, craftspeople, singers, musicians, comedians, lovers, friends, fathers, mothers, and humans.

Atrophy also happens with our spaces. Even spaces that are designed to serve us well, meet our needs, give us pleasure, and increase our joy can atrophy. When spaces are no longer useful to us, or they no longer inspire us, it affects the way we work and live and play in those spaces.

Have you ever watched a television show where a space is cleaned up, decluttered, reinvented, remodeled, or reimagined? Of course, you have. This kind of show is a multi-million-dollar business. We love watching spaces change. We love watching people experience joy. We feel joy with them. We love the "move that bus" moments where the *after-space* is revealed.

The *before spaces* are the *atrophied spaces*. The spaces became boring, or outdated, or not technologically advanced, or full of junk, or the kids moved out and the spaces no longer serve a purpose. They're full of objects that have atrophied as well. The treadmill in the corner is now a clothes hanger. The ripped sofa is now a folding table. The broken 1970s console television is now a bookshelf (but not in a cool way).

Space Atrophy is usually a gradual decline. In many cases, the space made sense for one reason or another at some point in the distant past. As we go through our lives and experience changes around us, many of us neglect changing our space along with our lifestyle and needs. Like the fish that doesn't know it's wet, if we aren't paying close attention, we will one day find ourselves in our spaces asking, "How did it come to this?"

Even if the space made sense at one time, in many cases it made sense from a purely *functional* point of view. Spaces are often designed with places to put our stuff—our furniture, our books, our clothes, our tools. Seldom do we ask, "Where do I want this space to *take* me?"

Can you start to imagine spaces as places that birth new things in you? Can you start to think of spaces as places that breathe life into you? Can you imagine your spaces as places that people stand in and think, "Wow. This place is special!" I hope so.

Idea Mentalists need to think of spaces as boutiques—that special place you go to get that special something that no one else has.

Take a minute. Wherever you are. Look around. Is the space you are in useful to you? Is it helping you accomplish what you need? Is it inspiring? Does it have personal items and things that bring you delight? Is it colorful? Do you like the colors? Is there enough light for you? If the space you are currently in is not giving you satisfactory answers to these questions, and you have the ability to change it, change it.

If you are frustrated by your space, it has atrophied. Think of your space as a living thing. If that living thing has atrophied, it is dead.

Dead Space.

It will start to suck the life out of you if it hasn't already.

Idea Mentalists are always making sure they stay on top of atrophy. With their minds. Their skills. Their experiences. Their education. And, their spaces.

Space Flight

I realize not everyone has the ability and/or permission to do what I'm about to suggest, but I still think there is a glimmer of hope here for everyone no matter their current restrictions. And, here it is . . . *if you can't change your workspace, change the space you work in.*

I realize many aspiring Idea Mentalists work in factories, hospitals, machinery shops, and other environments where changing the space you work in is not an option. Neither is it an option for you to work offsite. If you are in that spot, think of everything I'm going to suggest as being applicable to your private time—the time you carve out to breathe and think and dream.

Space flight comes in many different shapes and sizes. Let's focus on four kinds of Space Flight that can prove helpful for the ambitious Idea Mentalist: *Uncommon Space, Hiding Space, Spirit Space,* and *Inner Space.*

Uncommon Space

It was sometime in early 2009, and I was about to write my first self-published book. I love the process of writing, but for some reason I felt very uninspired. I looked around the space that I usually occupied for writing and studying and teaching and counseling and brainstorming and . . . I realized my problem. My space had become many things. Because it had become many things, it always felt like work when I was in it—the *distracting* kind of work. I couldn't detach and write because I was staring at the other icons and monuments related to my other responsibilities. Even though my space felt inspiring to others who walked into it, and I generally felt comfortable working in it, it was not conducive to my new goal, which was to write a book.

I asked myself the question, "Where do I feel inspired?" The answer was easy for me—nature. And, how did I usually get out and enjoy nature? Our motorhome. That was the answer I was looking for. I told my wife I would be working offsite in our motorhome for a few days, and I drove off on my *space voyage*.

Our motorhome at that time was an old 30' Pace Arrow with an onboard generator, a refrigerator, a stove, and propane heat. It was the beginning of winter in Michigan, so heat was a necessity. All the other accoutrements made it possible for me to create a fully stocked, functional, and inspiring space. I had never really looked at it as a writing retreat center before that day. Armed with my computer, a stocked fridge, and copious amounts of coffee, I started calling campgrounds to see where I might be able to park *The Traveling Parallelogram* (our pet name for our RV).

All the campgrounds were closed for the winter. But that didn't stop me. I just needed a good nature spot that I wasn't used to. So, I found myself parking *Arvie* (our other pet name for our RV) in the middle of a city park by the pond. For the next few days, I would wander outside to occasionally greet the birds and ducks who were still around, the squirrels, and the deer. It was too cold for anyone else to really enjoy the park, so I had the whole thing to myself for days.

Uncommon Space. The RV wasn't usually designated as a creative space or an office or a writing retreat. But, for those special days in that city park, it became all those things. I don't know how to explain this phenomenon to you, but Uncommon Space makes you think differently. It's like writing a song on a new instrument.

The RV experience was so rich for me that I still make a habit of creating Uncommon Space to think creatively and generate ideas. Other Uncommon Spaces I have tried on for size are borrowing a friend's cabin, staying in a friend's guestroom, setting up a space in my backyard, making a picnic desk by the river, driving our Airstream *Sundance* (the latest RV iteration) into the woods, renting an Airbnb, using a room at a friend's office, and renting a hotel room for a few days.

Hiding Space

I don't want it to sound like bragging, but I know a lot of people in my town. I love it. I love them. I've made it my goal to get to know a lot of people. But, true confessions, when I am in idea-mode and I'm on a roll, there are few things more annoying than having people come talk to you every two minutes. I don't have a great poker face, so I'm afraid they start to sense my frustration as well. This is a bad place for me to put myself in because I love people so much. Knowing this about myself, I need to plan my space accordingly.

Sometimes, creativity is fueled by the energy of a people-filled space—especially if you are all working together toward a common goal with great participation. Other times, you just need a space to hide. Where no one knows you.

Your Hiding Space is probably at least an hour away. Even if you aren't a social butterfly, the chances you'll run into someone you know within a thirty-minute radius of your town are pretty high. There's always that run to Costco or that trip to that antique store or that special restaurant outside of town that is going to drop someone in your lap. So, I've found the hour-plus radius to be a good start.

Hiding Space doesn't *always* have to be vibey, but it helps— especially if it's a spot you'll frequent. It doesn't have to be conducive to meditation or contemplation—although I have quite a few places I can hide that help me connect with my inner Zen Master. It just has to be away from the things and the people that will interrupt you. It's as simple as that. Idea

Mentalists need to be able to occasionally detach from the noise of life, or at least the things that constantly distract—social media, phones, friends, and even family.

Some of my favorite Hiding Spaces have been a nursery café, a greasy spoon, a hotel bar, a tobacco shop, a bookstore, a tea garden, and a rooftop.

Spirit Space

When my grandfather died, my grandmother had a difficult time throwing any of his stuff away. I'm not just talking about his Chief of Police badge or his wedding ring. I mean his clothes (socks, underwear, shoes, pants, sweaters, jackets), his magazines, his books, the relics he had in boxes from his time as Chief of Police, and even his medications. She couldn't even dump his booze, even though she didn't drink. She couldn't give it away to my alcoholic father and I wasn't of drinking age yet (I wish I had it now. He had some good scotches). She felt like she was throwing *him* away if she threw away his stuff. Marie Kondo could not have convinced her to toss anything in those early days and probably would have pissed her off. She was grieving.

She didn't need to toss everything. No one would have expected that. She needed to get rid of his *insignificant* stuff. It wasn't beneficial to keep it where it cluttered everything and served no purpose. It wasn't helping her grieve properly with all the stagnant memories hanging around. She couldn't discern between the things that made total sense to keep because of memories and moments and the shirt my grandpa bought at the thrift store the week before. She struggled through tears as my family all told her, "It's just stuff." But, what no one gave my grandma credit for was the fact that the objects, items, trinkets, art, and possessions in our space have a certain energy. The truth is, those sweaters made her feel his presence, and I understand why it was hard to let go. She was living in a time capsule that had great significance to her and she couldn't understand why people didn't get that. It wasn't healthy to keep it all, but she wasn't crazy.

I have another friend who tells me he does spring cleaning every year in his home. His home is full of more art, collections, souvenirs, and curiosities than I have seen anywhere. His home is like a museum of magical whimsy. When he comes across something during spring cleaning that he can't remember where it came from or why he has it, he gives it away. My friend sees his novelties as *stories*. When the thing no longer has a story attached to it, he gets rid of it. I wish I had this language back when we were helping grandma purge the insignificant stuff. I wish we could have helped her salvage and celebrate the stories. I think she would have understood. I think it would have helped her. I've adopted this mentality.

I'm a story collector. My stories have been on display in many different iterations of my Spirit Space. All these stories give me life. They talk to me and say, "You are loved." "You are part of a community." "YOU have a story to tell." My collections of stories include such things as art created by friends, a tobacco pipe collection curated from all over the world during my travels and marking special occasions, and pewter stirrup cups.

Some have mocked me for my collections of *stories* because of the room they occupy in my space. I've heard everything from, "When are you going to clean up?" to "You can't take it with you," and "It's all gonna burn one day." Well, the naysayers can kiss my butt. And, truth be told, *most people* get it. Most people walk in my spaces I've created and dream of having a similar space of their own.

I think one of the best ways to realize your need for Spirit Space is when you walk into a space that fills you. When you feel it, you feel it. When I light my favorite candle and put on a vinyl record in my Spirit Space as the rain is coming down, my mind ignites. All the stories begin to whisper to me. Some of the best ideas I've ever had have been forged in my Spirit Space.

Not everyone has the ability to create Spirit Space at their place of work. Not everyone wants it there. Is there a place in your home you can turn into Spirit Space? Is there a place in your yard—even a corner that's not being used that you can turn into Spirit Space?

My wife and I have turned our entire yard into Spirit Space. Our entire tiny yard says, "This is a place to be filled, take it all in, dream, think, relax, breathe, entertain, and show hospitality." Most of the plants are edible around the yard—the landscaping constantly gives to us in more ways than one. My wife's homemade fountains create a soothing constant trickle of natural white noise. The scents of the flowers are intoxicating. The birds gather here. We have multiple hummingbird feeders for our tiny friends to gather. At times, I sit outside and remain still with a cup of coffee. I let my mind wander. More than one crazy idea has come from this intoxicating spirit space my wife has created. I am currently sitting in this space next to a small bonfire, writing while I smoke a pipe.

I have a friend that lives in a small space. In the corner of her bedroom is a table and chair. A candle, a coffee cup, a journal, a blanket, and an essential oil diffuser also occupy the space by the bright window. Her Spirit Space. Here, she dreams, plans, and works out the ideas in her head. Spirit Space doesn't have to be like my atelier. It doesn't have to be surrounded by an edible landscape. It doesn't have to be full. It doesn't have to be stark. It has to be like YOU.

Another friend of mine does most of his idea-ing in an old English pub that smells like old tapestries, leather, stale cigarettes, and booze. He sits in a bulky wooden booth that's secluded beneath the mounted head of a six-point buck.

Think of your Spirit Space as that space you need to escape to because you feel most like you when you're there. Doesn't it make sense that ideas will come more readily in a space where you feel comfortable and inspired? Doesn't it make sense that ideas will come to you when you are the least distracted by the things that suck energy from you?

Inner Space

Inner Space is the most esoteric of all the spaces because it's all about contentment. Ultimately, only you can identify and nurture contentment. When everything around us changes, we need to be content with ourselves.

Get ready for something both coincidental and ironic. Between the last sentence you just read in the paragraph above and the lines you are currently reading, I got fired. I wrote those words on a Monday and got fired on a Wednesday. When I came back to start writing again, I had to laugh at the last thing I wrote.

The whole experience looking back was a train wreck, but this is the best reason I can come up with if I had to boil it down to one thing . . . It was because of my *ideas*.

My most recent employer was not ready for them. I was hired for my ideas, and ironically fired for them. My ideas clashed with the ideas of some others on staff who had a more conservative idea of how things should be and that's where it all started to go haywire.

Many of the people who benefited from my ideas loved them. The town loved them. My ideas over the few years in that work environment were far more loved and celebrated than they were not. But, your ideas won't work for everyone. Maybe it's the culture. Maybe it's the timing. Maybe someone fears your ideas. There are a number of reasons why your ideas might be rejected.

When you wake up in the morning and your feet hit the floor, even before your first cup of coffee, you need to be confident that YOU ARE AN IDEA MENTALIST. The world needs your ideas. Maybe not in the current climate. Maybe not with the current team. Maybe not at this time. You are still you. Six days after I was let go, I wrote this poem, below.

THE SONG

You put it out there
Unembellished soul
Defenseless truth
Do you dare to speak the whole?

A sing-able chorus
An approachable chime
For those who will hear it
It will stand the test of time

The sweat in the melody
The hours in the rhyme
The commitment to the craft
In every single line

Some will sing its praises
They'll pass it to their friends
Some are moved to tears
Swearing that it mends

Some won't understand it
Some will speak against it
Some will try to stifle it
Some will try to censor it

Some will say they love it
Until someone claims distaste
Then they'll say, "I've never liked it"
Changing sentiments in haste

Some will judge it harshly
Because they think it is their right
Some will call it evil
Burn your record in the night

Some will wait for others
To tell them if it's good or bad
Having no taste of their own
Following every trend and fad

Some will only listen
To the music of the youth
And they'll miss out on the old souls
The depth, the pain, the truth

Some will hear it faintly
And they'll say they understand
But, to hear is not to listen
So, their judgements all wax bland

Some will come to hear your song
And sit in the front row
With a smile on their face
As you bleed throughout the show

Ah, but when the show is over
Or, perhaps they choose to leave
Don't be at all surprised
When their criticisms you read . . .

"Scandalous! Unruly!"
The title of their review

The very same critics
Who once proclaimed the ballad as truth

Some despise the poet prophet
Especially one who wields a pen
Or performs at nighttime galas
Or draws the people in

Some hate the music mystic
They label their verse "sorcery"
They hold everything inside
And fear those who say it openly

Some hate the preacher protestor
They prefer to stay naive
"Don't sing out against injustice . . .
Or our patrons, they might leave!"

Some just want an easy song
Downloaded for free
Sing-songy and clap-able
On the one and three

Some are frightened of the tune
That threatens to convict
They'd rather hear a pretty lie
That turns into a hit

So, beware if you desire
Or feel "called" to write a song
Get used to feeling naked
Before an unpredictable throng

The dead writers scream,
"If you sell out and fail to tell the truth . . .
That is burning in your bones . . .
Even if it is uncouth . . .

If you cut your hair so the "respectable"
Will be more likely to hear your song . . .
Know that you are not the writer
You thought you were all along."

So, clutch your pen and sketchpad
For the ears that want to hear
Embrace the limericks and explicit lines
The simple-minded fear

There's a people famished for a song
That cuts right to the heart
And when that song is finished
Another's waiting for you to start

I wrote that poem as a testament and love poem to me
and others who have been deeply wounded by some that
disdain our ideas and make it personal. Ideas are dangerous
commodities. Some folks feel deeply threatened by your ideas.
And they turn on you.

A friend told me a long time ago that there are two ways to
have the biggest building in town—you build yours taller, or
you tear all the other ones down. When he spoke of buildings,
he was talking about what happens on the *inside*.

Some call Inner Space your *soul*. That may be a good word.
Others say your mind and heart are all part of Inner Space, but
I don't know that I'd get too carried away with the delineations.
Close your eyes and hear yourself breathe. What's on your
mind? Can you feel your pulse? Hear your heart? Your breath?
Are you aware of your humanity? All of this is part of your
Inner Space.

It can't be neglected. It needs to be fed. Dietary choices,
exercise, meditation, prayer, the pursuit of God and spirituality,
rest, pampering yourself, volunteering, generosity, pets,

nature, children, decluttering, yoga, massages, self-education, stargazing, gardening . . . all of these things are often talked about when it comes to food for your soul. I highly recommend most of them (I have yet to get a taste for yoga).

Inner Space is a spot you nurture inside yourself that helps you withstand the blows of the nay-sayers. And guess what? No one has permission to rent your Inner Space unless you let them in. No one gets to dictate how you adorn your Inner Space. No one can share it unless you invite them.

CHAPTER SEVEN
IT'S A PLAY THING

Pliny's Plight

I don't know if it's true or not but, I once heard that the Roman author Pliny the Elder (and you thought it was just a good beer) was such a workaholic that he had servants feed him while he worked—just opened up and said, "Ahhh."

My guess is he was applauded.

"Way to go, Pliny!"
"Man, that Pliny is a hard worker!"
"Why can't you be like your brother Pliny?"
"I wish I had the dedication of Pliny."

Here's the thing about being addicted to work: It's the easiest addiction to hide, because the more *successful* you are and the harder you work, the more people sing your praises. And . . . praise is incredibly addicting.

Please allow me to go down a rabbit hole for a bit about **workaholism** before we climb back out and talk about the importance of play and how play can release the Idea Mentalist inside you that is scratching you up from the inside waiting to be released. This chapter is one of the most important in this book. Because, the art of play is dying for many people and many organizations. As such, Idea Mentalists are dying before they're even born.

I think having a good work perspective is healthy. I got my good work perspective from my dad. He taught me to work hard, take care of our tools, and have a heart of gratitude while you're doing whatever it is you do. He taught me that work will always be hard no matter what you do. *The sweat has to come from somewhere.* My dad has that Bruce Springsteen work ethic—the kind that believes hard work has a moral component to it. Hard work benefits humankind and it is healing for your soul.

As I was growing up, my dad never took a handout unless it was the last possible option he thought he had. He worked a bunch of what we called "Joe Jobs" (any average Joe could work them) when work was not there. I remember one time my dad took me fishing when there was no work coming in. It was cold outside. We had no good fishing gear to speak of. We didn't know what we were doing. We caught nothing. But, my dad was willing to try and willing to do anything to feed his family. That kind of work perspective is pretty amazing. That is not workaholism. That is responsibility.

I think a good definition for workaholism is, "A toxic and futile compulsion to constantly do more work." My name is John. I'm a workaholic.

Maybe I got the disease as a member of Generation X. The MTV generation. The forgotten generation. The don't-label-me generation. Maybe I got it in college because I went back later than most of my friends and had something to prove. Maybe I got it because I watched my dad suffer to make a living, and now I don't want to be poor. Maybe I contracted it when I worked in financial services and got a taste for blood while chasing the almighty dollar. I think maybe all of those scenarios added to my addiction, along with an unhealthy dose of guilt and the feeling that I'm not doing enough.

It's a mess, honestly. I have to fight to not work hard. I've been in counseling to combat it. I have Life Editors that speak into me and help me not be what I am often unhealthily compelled to be.

Maybe you don't know you are one. Maybe you see it in someone else. Here are some ways to define workaholism that I have learned from my counselors and experience. They aren't all 100% true for everyone, but when is that ever the case? Some of us have a bit of all these signs. Some of us have them all in spades. Like a shovel. We have it in scoopfuls.

Performance: Workaholics are often addicted to achieving something that is beyond what anyone expects of them. The problem with this (I know firsthand) is that when you are a high-level achiever and get more accomplished than anyone on your team and do huge things that blow minds—more than what anyone expects of a normal human being—it becomes your *new standard*. People start wondering what's wrong with you when you aren't setting new standards of excellence.

But, it's not really excellence we're after as workaholics. It's perfection. This is toxic. We desperately want to appear faultless, so we work twice as much to make sure there is less chance of a chink in our armor.

Drive: I really enjoy my work. I get to do a variety of things and have a lot of permission. SOME workaholics don't enjoy their work. They just feel a need to be working. All the time. It's like work possesses them—in that *Exorcist* kind of way. This is way different than someone who is motivated, or someone who's a self-starter, or simply a hard worker. Workaholics often have a voice in their heads telling them they aren't doing enough. They *should* be working MORE.

Sometimes, the drive comes from a space deep inside where we live with some feeling of incompetence in another area of our lives that we don't feel like we have control over. So we WORK to compensate for the area we feel incompetent or useless or ineffective.
By the way, if you work in an intense, fast-paced, demanding career, it doesn't mean you are or will become a workaholic. However, if you are a workaholic and that is your work environment, it certainly doesn't help.

Brain space: Workaholics often think about work. Even when they aren't working. They justify why they need to be thinking about it. Their friends and family know work is always on their mind. They can't hide it. They have a hard time flipping off the work switch. Oftentimes, they can't go on vacation and enjoy it. They don't take breaks. They rent out every available space in their heads to work.

Emotional baggage: If you're a workaholic, you might feel guilty when you aren't working. This has been a big one for me. I've dealt with it my whole life. I literally have felt like people are watching me if I take a break. I've announced to everyone why I am not working at the time. I've asked my family for permission to not work around the home even if they don't put pressure or expectations on me. I've fought depression when not working. I've contended with anxiety when not working. Nothing says we're having fun at Disneyland like, "Dad's depressed that he's not working." Nothing says *this is a great lunch date* like, "Mom's anxiety is through the roof because she can't not look at her work phone."

Sometimes, workaholics have deeper emotional issues from scars of the past, our family of origin, or maybe work is a coping mechanism to not feel the pain. Guilt, anger, disappointment, the fear of disappointing—they can all contribute.

PS . . . trust me. It can get better. I wish I could go back and talk to 1995 Workaholic John and tell him what I've learned. But, in all honesty it took time for me to learn.

Personality: Not all science agrees with this, but if you've ever done a Myers-Briggs profile or worked with the Enneagram, it's hard not to recognize how personality seems to steer us. Understanding our personality tendencies can be helpful in avoiding pitfalls.

This doesn't mean personality types give us an excuse to treat people cruelly or act one way or the other. I worked with a guy one time who was not nice to people. I called him on it one day

and he said, "You and I just have different personality types."
To which I responded, "Asshole is not a personality type."

I look at it like diabetes. I have to control my adult-onset
diabetes with my diet. Thankfully, I am not on insulin at this
point in my life. I used to think diabetes was something only
overweight people got. My doctor tells me this is not true.
Also, my tiny little niece has Type 1 diabetes, so I KNOW it's
not all about weight. However, if you have diabetes, it's not a
good idea to have *extra weight*.

The more real estate you carry around, the harder it is to
control your diabetes. So, what does this have to do with
personality? If you are a Type A personality, or ENTJ, or
a "1" on the Enneagram, those things do not MAKE you a
workaholic. Knowing the strengths and weaknesses of those
personality types can help you manage your workaholism. The
more personality type WEIGHT you carry, the harder it is to
manage the disease.

A Story About Trophies and Stuff

We were making a move across the country. While sorting into
two piles—the "keep pile" and the "oh-my-gosh-we-need-to-
rent-a-dumpster-pile"—I came across a box marked "Trophies"
and took the next half-hour to walk down memory lane. In
my early twenties, I sold life insurance and it was this well-
respected-by-many profession (enter laugh here) that provided
me the opportunity to collect many well-deserved plastic
monuments to my success. There was the trophy I earned for
becoming the youngest Vice President. There was the engraved
clock I received for having the highest production rate of any
office in our region. There was the promotion plaque.

Then I remembered the other mementos of my illustrious
career in insurance—the ulcers, the headaches, the fights with
my wife, and the constant emotional struggle to stay on top.

I have many other friends with a similar story . . .

A friend of mine works at a large computer company. Twenty-five years ago, we were hanging out and he told me they had purchased brand new laptops as a "gift" for every one of their 7,000 employees at his work campus. Everyone was thrilled. Free computer!

His corporation didn't get to be as big as they are by being stupid. Productivity in their division increased by at least 25% to 30% in his estimation because of everyone bringing their laptops home and working at night. They would log in "just to check email" and end up working themselves to sleep.

The disturbing trend was perpetuated by managers high-fiving their employees for their work ethic. More production meant bigger bonuses and so on and so on and so on.

Workaholism does not affect anyone differently because of gender. It's certainly not a man's thing. As a matter of fact, I think some women have a tougher go of it. A lot of career women I meet and coach feel the same pressure to produce and get ahead and make something of themselves, but simultaneously feel this innate desire to keep the family in order. As if raising a family isn't hard enough, they have two battlefields they fight on.

I was visiting a friend whose wife worked at a large corporation. During dinner, she checked her email to find that her boss was in a "tough spot" on a Sunday, during dinner. She couldn't bear the thought of not answering his email. She felt soooo bad. I jokingly said to her, "Poor bossy-poo. Poor boss that makes three million a year." I spent some time with her, asking about her obsession, and she admitted that it felt good for someone to recognize her efforts—something that wasn't happening at home.

All the workaholism warning signs have something in common . . . *identity* and *control*.

A Story About Identity and Control

There's an interesting story about identity and control in the Bible. Whatever you think about the biblical narrative—even if you think the stories are just a myth or metaphor, or if you think the whole thing is a joke—there are some interesting stories from a pure literary perspective.

As the story goes, Adam (the Biblical first man) lost his *identity* in the Garden of Eden—or at least lost sight of it. His identity was originally as a child of the Deity. Complete. Adam had it all, but the story says he threw it away. Adam, who once knew God as his center—the place he found life—and knew God as the controller and sustainer of everything, decided to thrust himself into the center and try to become like God. Adam made a *control* move. "I'm in control here! I say who I am and who I want to be." He realized he was in control of his destiny. No one could stop him. If he wanted to eat the fruit, he could. And he did. Adam (and the rest of humanity, according to the story) spent the rest of his life struggling to gain acceptance, trying to make something of himself, trying to regain his identity, and trying to prove himself. The potent warning in the context of the Bible story is that the misplaced identity and control move affected all of Adam's *relationships* because they were rooted in selfishness.

Chasing dreams, being the best version of ourselves, making and reaching goals . . . I'm all for it. Wanting control and wanting worth are not bad in and of themselves either. But, when the desire to control absolutely everything in our lives, without acknowledging how it affects others, and without acknowledging we are not in *complete* control, and/or when we let *what we do* define us . . . this is where it all goes whackadoodle.

Some of us have a greedy drive to work hard because we want to be in control of everything and everyone at all costs. Some of us have a drive because we want worth, and we find that worth by comparing ourselves to others and detracting and devaluing the worth in them.

Sometimes, we feel worth when our lifestyle is better than someone else's. Sometimes, we feel worth when we accomplish something greater than the next person. We might feel worth when someone attaches worth to us because they have judged our performance against someone else's or against our previous performance. Sometimes our love for our fellow human becomes shrouded and eclipsed by our desire for control and identity. It's all about *me*. Work becomes our drug. Our addiction.

Selling insurance all those years ago fueled my workaholism for sure. When you are a driver in the life insurance industry, you make a sale whenever you can. Day or night. And, my company had huge incentives. Money. Position. Trips. Accolades. When I used to sell insurance, my favorite mantras used to include such things as "I have it because I wanted it more than you," and other self-serving, pithy grabbers and proverbial catch phrases. I would be quick to preach hard work, but patience was seldom mentioned. I was quick to point out the benefits of determination, but wisdom was ignored. My goals were always focused on "me" achieving what "I" wanted (of course, I disguised it by the way I worded them and talked about them, but "I" was the bottom line).

After years of heartache as a slave to work. . . I altered my philosophy of working and goal setting in the *what for* and the *who for* categories. Each and every goal I set—whether it is physical, social, financial, educational, spiritual, vocational, or recreational— I want to be a goal set in light of things that last. I want to ask the question "What difference will this make (for my wife, my kids, my grandkids, my city, and the world) after I'm gone?" Some would call this a *legacy*.

Our legacy, for some of us, will be how we trained our children about work and what lasts and what has value. Work is not a curse. There can be joy in it. It is not only necessary to prevent poverty and destitution—it can be rewarding. Responsibility and care *for others* through labor is natural. When that work *takes the place of people* and love—it gets ugly. Don't run the risk of becoming tunnel-vision at the expense of relationships.

Killing Workaholism

We are not what we do. We are not our ideas. Really, at our core, we are not Idea Mentalists. I have had a bunch of jobs that put food on the table over the last thirty plus years— cabinet maker, painting contractor, hod carrier, women's shoes salesman, pastor, financial services rep, touring musician, and business owner. But at my CORE, I am none of those things. I don't have to strive to be something I am not. I need to live in the reality of who I am. We are all human beings who live, work, and play among other humans that matter. Know this. Live this.

Here are some good questions to ask ourselves when goal setting and examining our workload in light of what matters for our legacy:

Is this thing on my work list still a priority or do I just want to carry it over so I can eventually cross it off my list?

Have circumstances changed recently that should cause me to reevaluate this work goal, pass it on to someone else, or cross it off altogether?

Is this task realistic in light of my current responsibilities?
If I take it on, can I do it with excellence (notice I didn't say perfection)?

If I ran this work item past my wife or my trusted friend first, would they have some things to say about it?

Will I have to give up something in order to achieve this goal?

Could there be a "bigger yes" that should cause me to say "no" to this at this time?

Will this work situation rob me of my time or money to be generous to others?

Have I tried this before and felt like I failed? What has changed to make me want to attempt it again?

Will anyone be disappointed in me for adding this to the list?

If someone I trust took a big red pen to my goal sheet, what comments would they make in the margins?

Finally, take time to rest. Rest is part of the workaholism cure. Enable your off-switch. I've found this is one of the hardest things to do in my life.

It's not only hard because *you or I* have a hard time unwinding and letting go. It's hard because it can seem like *everyone else* has a hard time letting us unwind and let go. Maybe you find yourself taking a vacation for a week and the next thing you know, everybody is saying things like "Huh, must be nice!" "How long were you going to stay away?" I've found that people don't really like it when I rest.

In ancient Jewish culture, the days of the week had no names. They were known only by their ordinal numbers. The only one that has a name is the Shabbat (or, the Sabbath). It's the day of rest. And, it's the climax of the week.

The workaholic is not a religious hero in Judaism.

Some Practical Tips to Fight Workaholism

- Leave that computer at work.
- Leave at the same time every day.
- Plan annual play with the special people in your life. Calendar playdates.
- Save money just for play. *I have a separate bank account for play.*
- Be still. Be quiet. Be honest with the thoughts inside your head.
- Plan and calendar for *you time*. Take baths. Walk. Play music. Make art. Do whatever floats your boat.
- Find a Life Editor—a person who will cut through the lies you tell yourself with love and truth.
- Seek counsel. Ask for advice.
- Have a talk with your boss about your workaholism. Tell them about the statistics of burnout, high blood pressure, heart attack, and depression. If you are a workaholic, your boss probably knows it and while they like your productivity, they also don't want blood on their hands.
- Practice gratitude. Make a list of the simple things you are thankful for—especially the things you didn't make happen. Be observant of the things that are beautiful without your influence. Enjoy those things.

Play All the Time

I expect by now we are all cured of our workaholism because I did such a good job in this chapter thus far (that's sarcasm, kids). What I'm about to suggest now is not just a cure for workaholism, it's a way of life that lightens burdens and increases joy. It's the life blood of an Idea Mentalist. I already gave it away. **Play. All the time.**

My wife stopped asking me the question "Is everything a game to you?" years ago. Because she knows the answer. Yes. It absolutely is. I find joy in the small things. I see friendly competition where others see everyday tasks. I make songs out of everyday conversation. I see unsanctioned time trials where others see chores. There's too much to celebrate about life to allow the mundane to become burdensome.

Play is another thing I learned from my dad. While some bosses are fond of saying things like, "Quit playing and get to work," my dad blurred the lines. He sang while slinging paint on a ladder, he danced as he sprayed lacquer on cabinets, and he made contests out of paintbrush cleaning.

The science behind the benefits of play is well documented. Do a Google search for any combination of the word *play* with the words *science*, *adult*, *brain*, and/or *benefits* and you can spend hours reading articles about the benefits of play for your health and creativity.

However, knowing the benefits of play cognitively and *experiencing* the results of play as an Idea Mentalist are vastly different.

There is probably only a very small percentage of us that think play is frivolous. Most humans enjoy a good vacation, a walk in the woods, floating on a pontoon boat, a casual bike ride, or tossing a ball with our children or grandchildren. But, a larger percentage of us would have a hard time including play *in our work routine* unless it had some benefit such as competition with the promise of reward.

The Idea Mentalist must be willing to try on play for size. During meetings. During work routines. In the middle of traffic jams. While cleaning the house.

Playing Around

The following is a list of playful activities I have found helpful for fresh, innovative thinking and idea generation over the years.

Blogging and writing: I know what you're thinking. Blogs seem passé. So 2005. About fifteen years ago, I saw a woman wearing a shirt that said, "No one cares about your blog." But, you don't need to blog with the hopes of attracting 100,000 readers a day or building a platform in order to monetize your site.

Think of blogging as the postmodern-day diary. Write for you. Get your thoughts out. Listen to yourself talk. Explore the trails your thoughts take and find your written voice. Say what you want to say. Say what you feel.

I don't know that you've thought of it this way, but social media sites are forms of blogging—micro-blogging to be exact. If you're not a 300-600 word daily blogger, consider micro-blogging as a way to carefully and thoughtfully craft what's on your mind.

Make stuff: Do you work with wood? Paint? Sculpt? Weld? Whittle? Carve? Design spaces? Have you always wanted to start one of those things but haven't taken the time?

The Idea Mentalist creates *just because*. My wife is a pro at this. She always has a project she is making. It's not unusual for me to be gone for a couple of days and come home to a house that has been rearranged, freshly painted walls, new pillows that she's sewn, and decorative shelving where there once was a painting. Not only does this make our living space feel like it's alive, but also my wife stays sharp in the process. The last few years we've lived in very small spaces. Just when I think we've maximized our storage capabilities, she finds a way to make art that doubles as storage. The bigger payoff is that my wife gets energy and new ideas by being playful and making stuff in our spaces.

What do you do with that branch that just fell off your tree? Some throw it in the green bin. Others bore holes for candles and make a centerpiece. What do you do with that kitchen sink you just replaced? Some throw it in the trash. Others install it in the backyard on a potting bench. What do you do with that old painting you bought at Michaels twenty years ago and have since realized was a bad decision? Some donate it to Goodwill. Others see a good canvas and paint over it.

Voice memos: Everyone talks to themselves. Some talk inside their own heads. Some of us talk out loud. Idea Mentalists talk out loud and sometimes record themselves talking.

As a songwriter, singing freestyle melodies into my iPhone has been a common, helpful, playful practice for me. I have countless voice memos on my phone. Some of them are embarrassing. Some of them have led to some of my favorite songs.

It's not just melodies that I record. Poems. Jokes. Thoughts. Phrases. Ideas. Memoirs. Confessions. Dreams.

Toys and games: My atelier in Michigan was my greatest toy and game layout to date, and the time I occupied the space was arguably my most creative and innovative decade yet. A chess board sat out at all times. The shelves were stacked with role-playing games and trivia games. My desk was full of action figures and figurines from cult television shows. Mind-teasing puzzles were everywhere. #nerd

My friend David, who shared the space with me, is also a collector of toys and games and has a penchant for making steampunk weapons. As a matter of fact, I'm quite sure it was David's love for toys and games that pushed me in this direction.

Did David and I play with all the toys? No. I hate chess. I get wearied with role-playing games faster than I can unpack their 10,000 pieces and multiple sets of cards. But, there was no mistaking that our environment was one full of *permission to play*.

Permission. That's what an Idea Mentalist needs. Surrounding yourself with playful things is a visual reminder that you have permission. Nobody puts Baby in a boring corner.

Fiction February: It's easy to get wrapped up in a constant barrage of recommended books on how to increase sales, be a better manager, know your strengths, and manage your time better. It's easy to constantly look for the next new book that will help you crack the code of self-improvement, think and work smarter, find satisfaction, grow spiritually, and/or improve your self-image. Shoot, the book you're reading now fits into at least one of the categories I just mentioned.

Conventional wisdom says that the above things will be accomplished by reading *non-fiction*. How-to books. Propositions. Guidelines. Statistics. Studies. Science. Business.

But, conventional wisdom often falls short. Ask yourself how many non-fiction books have changed you, moved you to tears, inspired you to love your children more, compelled you to hug your spouse, or caused you to question the trajectory of your life. There might be some.

Probably not many.

It's *stories* that move us.

The stories are where the real magic lies. There's magic in the compelling stories that get banned and burned. It's compelling stories that are feared by despots and zealots.

It's speeches like that of Samwise Gamgee given to Frodo Baggins on their journey to Mordor that make us want to keep going. When Aslan the Lion explains to Aravis that the pain he inflicted was to teach her empathy for the way she treated her stepmother's slave, we too question those we have hurt and the pain we've brought upon ourselves in the process. It was Orwell's words published in 1949 in his book, *1984,* that gave us the sentiment, "Big Brother is watching you"—words that have come back to haunt us and caused us to scramble to protect ourselves after we gave our identities, information, likes and dislikes away so freely in the internet age.

Every February, I put aside all books designed as how-to, steps-to, ways-to, why-for, laws-of, art-of, guide-to, and fundamentals-of. I read stories. I dare you to do the same. Mystery, romance, adventure, crime-drama, horror, fantasy—whatever niche you choose. Read it. Take it in. Escape. Involve yourself with the characters. Invest in the hero. Understand the villain. Identify with the plot and the subplots.

Role-play: No, I don't mean bedroom shenanigans. But by all means, knock yourself out.

I'm referring to conversation between comrades where you take on someone else's persona (e.g., a boss, a spouse, an authority figure, a client) in an effort to face your fears, understand someone, face opposition, get ahead of controversy, vet ideas for initial feedback, problem solve, and build confidence.

When I was barely twenty-two and in the financial services industry, I would role-play with my office buddies all the time.

It helped me develop strategies that proved to be incredibly helpful and catapulted me to become one of the top sales agents not only in my office but in the country. Role-playing helped me develop stories that I would share with clients to help develop a camaraderie and trust. Role-playing gave me ideas for problem solving. Role-playing encouraged me to get ahead of controversy and diffuse bombs before giving someone else the chance to light one off.

Years ago, I teamed up with a friend and pitched him an idea to make a charity wine. My friend John is a vintner, vineyard owner, and a craftsman. He loved the idea. The only problem was, we were in a conservative town in the Midwest—not exactly the hotbed of forward thinking. To up the ante, I was working for a church and wanted the church to be the main sponsor. Not all churches are created equal, but there are very few of them that would take on a project where they'd invest in alcohol for resale.

My vintner friend and I wanted to give the money to a struggling art school that hosted after-school programs for children whose parents didn't have the means to pay for the programs. Honestly, at this school, there weren't many parents in the picture at all.

I shared the idea with one trusted friend before launching the whole campaign, and his face went blank. He told me it was a beautiful idea, but I should prepare myself for "the controversy." I was no stranger to controversy as an unconventional church leader and an Idea Mentalist. I took his advice to get some good thinkers in a room and toss around possible pushback to get ahead of the controversy.

For a couple of hours, I sat in a room with men and women, friends of mine, who are community leaders, teachers, business owners, and politicians. The first part of the meeting was surfacing their concerns and casting vision for the project. The conversation was a test of my patience at times. I'm an early adopter and I'm allergic to religious conservatism (the kind where every new idea is suspect).

I have anxiety attacks in a *culture of fear*. For what seemed like an eternity, the group I had assembled was helping me live my worst nightmare. Then it dawned on me: these people were my friends. They were actually on my side. If someone is going to help you get ahead of controversy, who is better to do that than your friends? I realized that my friends were helping me in huge ways by being honest about their own concerns first. If they, the people who loved and respected me, had concerns and wanted the project to be successful, then surely there were going to be people with the same concerns who didn't care about me or the project at all.

Then something happened. The tone of the conversation changed, or, at least, I perceived a change. Perhaps it was just a change in my perspective, but I suddenly realized I had a room full of cheerleaders. A conversation that started out with a defensive tone (or, at least that's how it felt to me) suddenly sounded helpful and encouraging. Role-playing became fun and . . . well . . . playful.

My friends started putting themselves in the roles of people in the community and started asking questions like, "What will the outspoken pastor of the little Baptist church say?" "What will the conservative parents say?" "What will the media say?" "What will the AA group that meets at the church say?" And, as these questions were raised, my friends helped me count the cost of the potential controversy. We crafted statements and responses and good answers for the objections that might surface as I cast vision to the general public.

I began meeting with some folks in the community that we recognized might need a little TLC and forecasting before we launched into the project. I met with local pastors. I met with some in the media. I met with some key parent leaders. Finally, I met with the local AA group and told them the story. The AA group became one of the biggest fans of the project and they encouraged me to move forward. I'll never forget how they helped me craft language and told me stories of how they believed "alcohol and alcoholism are two different things."

That little meeting of role-playing helped me tell a compelling story to the community through radio, television, and social media before the wine was even for sale. I told a story of wine as art that would in turn help young artists. I told a story of a local vintner doing something selfless as he used his skills to raise money for children in desperate need. I told a story of how a broken economy could and would rise from the ashes as long as there were people willing to lend a hand to humanity.

We made the wine. We sold the wine. We raised nearly $10,000 for the school. We became the largest single donor to the art school that year. And, we did it with *barely a peep* from the cautious and conservative community. There were a couple of militant naysayers, for sure, but they rose and fell quickly.

Role-playing. I'm a fan.

Twoosh: When Twitter started, there was a 140-character limit for posts. Today, there is a 280-character limit. A twoosh is a Twitter post with exactly 280 characters—no more, no less. Crafting a twoosh can be a fun exercise in learning how to succinctly communicate what you want to say.

The last paragraph is a twoosh. Go on. You can count the characters if you'd like.

Twooshing is the kind of whimsical play that keeps the mind of an Idea Mentalist sharp. Twooshing can also temporarily lighten sorrows. It can be a much-needed break in your monotonous day. Start twoosh contests with your friends. Vet an idea through a twoosh. Challenge yourself.

The last paragraph was also a twoosh.

24^2: Some play takes more of an investment. Such is the case with the adventure game I created called 24 Squared (stylized as 24^2). This exercise can be done by yourself or with a group. I've always had more fun in a group—making it some kind of a contest. I talked about this earlier, but I'll mention the rules again.

Gather a few friends and head to a city you enjoy visiting. Make it an overnight trip. Roam the city—the parks, the museums, the coffee shops, the nightclubs, the malls, the quaint shops, the bike trails, the theaters, the galleries, and the restaurants. Take it all in. Observe. Pay attention. Listen. Engage. Take photos of all the great ideas you see. While engaging in 24^2, a great idea can come in many forms, such as art, design, food, drink, architecture, song, fashion, language, and customer service.

You must gather your best twenty-four ideas in a 24-hour period and share them with your friends. Talk about why the ideas grabbed your attention.

Do these twenty-four ideas inspire you to new ideas? Will you incorporate some of these ideas into your routine? Do these ideas compel you to change something that isn't working in your environment? Idea Mentalist, I dare you to play 24^2 and not be inspired.

Road games: Our family has always been a road trip kind of family. We've owned pop-up tent trailers, Class A RVs, travel trailers, and we camped in tents and backpacked once upon a younger time. We enjoy long drives to visit big cities. Every day can be a road trip if you view it through that lens.

The thing that makes a road trip feel like a road trip to us is the road games we play along the way. Sure, there are the standards like Road Bingo and the Alphabet Game, but there are also the dozens of games we've invented that make trips so exciting. Furthermore, we look at each road trip as an opportunity to invent *another* road game. One day, I'll write a book dedicated to road games. We have that many.

Games like, Do They Go with Their Car? What Does That Person Do for a Living? and What is His/Her Story? have provided hours of entertainment for our family, but they have also shaped my kids to be some of the wittiest, think-on-your-feet humans I've ever met.

The games I listed above are easy-access games. You don't have to be a road game rockstar to play them. But then there are the games that require a bit more skill. Games that are not for the weak. Games that challenge creativity to new levels.

Such is the case with a game we refer to as, Remember That Song? In this game, one person starts by challenging another in the group by asking, "Remember that song (insert name of fake song) by that band (insert name of fake band) from the (insert decade) that was kind of a (insert genre)? For the next minute or so, others chime in with fake details about the made-up song from the made-up band. Finally, the person being challenged says, "I totally remember it. It went like this . . ." and they sing the fake song.

My wife hates to play this game. She doesn't fancy herself a singer (although, you don't have to be good and that never really stopped the most horrid singers from doing karaoke). She likes to listen to me and the kids play, though. The game is not for everyone.

All of my kids excel at Remember That Song? But, my youngest is in a category all by herself. Kasidy cranks out hit songs on-the-fly like I imagine Taylor Swift writes her melodies or Elton John did when he cranked out seventeen full-length albums in his first ten years, not counting his Greatest Hits collections. One time, while playing this game on a trip in the eastern US, Kasidy actually made me cry with one of the fake ballads she sang. She didn't gravitate to the easy pop formulas or low-hanging-fruit rhyme schemes for her fake ballad. It was thoughtful. Emotional. Emotive.

Kasidy is an Idea Mentalist to a greater degree than many people three times her age—and not just with road games. She has ideas for everything. My other children are no slackers either. I'm convinced my kids are Idea Mentalists in large part because they have learned how to play well. They, like me, believe there's a song for everything, a contest for everyone, an inherent puzzle beneath the surface, and joy to be found in the mundane.

My kids' playfulness has made them so sharp that they get every job they apply for and quickly rise to the top as a star performer in whatever organization they are a part of. Managers and owners hate to see them go when they move on because they are the Idea Mentalists, inventors, problem solvers, flag wavers, cheerleaders, and purveyors of innovation that every organization dreams of. They increase productivity and profits and spread good cheer with every staff they have the opportunity to work with. And, they are most definitely the most playful workers ever.

If you want to crush my children as an employer, take away their freedom to innovate. Tell them to do things the way they've always been done, even if it's not the best way. Tell them to stop playing around and be serious. They'll soon move on from that company and gravitate toward a job with freedom and playfulness. That's what Idea Mentalists do. That's what I've always done. Maybe you have too. Maybe you will now.

Photo exercises: The Idea Mentalist thinks of modern-day conveniences in unconventional ways. For example, to the Idea Mentalist, the smartphone camera is not simply to capture moments. The camera is a *tool, an artist's instrument, an impression aggregator,* and a *game maker.*

One day, I walked around the historic district of my town with my camera in hand and took photos of every single historic marker I could find. They were everywhere. They were freestanding, on buildings, on the sidewalks, on pillars, on stone, and on bridges. I learned a ton about my city that morning while getting exercise. I have a list compiled now of potential ideas for my city that spawned from this walk—a historic storytelling tour, a history scavenger hunt, an art piece with impressions of all the markers, a recreation of all the markers to use as a wall-hanging, a series of short stories for children based on the locations . . . the list goes on.

On another morning, I took my phone on a walk and took photos of the ground as I walked. I seldom take the time to look at the ground when I'm walking, but this morning I took photos of the many different textures beneath my feet. The grass. The brick. The gravel. The sidewalk. The trail. The paint stains on the street. The wildflowers. The manhole covers. The storm drains. The concrete variations. The railroad tracks. The gum on the road.

I then arranged all the photos into a giant mosaic of color and texture, and wrote a blog post about noticing what beauty is beneath you and taken for granted. I compiled a list of ideas from this exercise. Some of the examples include an art auction made up of beneath-our-feet photos to raise money for cerebral palsy (in honor of my friend who cannot walk due to the disease), a story about the creatures who live in the lands beneath our feet, and a cleanup of the areas in my town to draw attention to the beauty there.

Will I ever embark on the ideas? I don't know. But, that's not really the point of playfulness. Playfulness is like advertising for the Idea Mentalist. One should never look at advertising as a direct connection to a sale. One can't spend $1,500 on an ad and wonder, "How many customers will I get from this ad?" Advertising doesn't work like that. Advertising is a long game. It's more about brand recognition, familiarity, trust, and keeping your brand at the forefront in everyone's mind. Advertising pays off, but usually in the long run. Over time. With consistency.

As it is with advertising, so is the same for playfulness. Playfulness helps you build idea-creating muscle memory, mental stamina, sharpness, wit, and intelligence.

Play the expert: There was a time in my life where I collected a lot of things. According to my wife, too many things. She was right. I had to scale back—especially when we downsized by over 4,000 square feet.

I don't collect things because I like clutter (although, my wife says I have a "pile-it license"). I collect things because I like to learn about them. In Chapter Five, I mentioned my tobacco pipe collection. I talked about the thrill of the acquisition and the many conversations I've had and connections I've made because of my pipes. I also like *learning* about pipes. Learning about things is a pathway to becoming an expert on things. Becoming an expert leads to interesting conversations with interesting people. Those conversations lead to relationships which lead to opportunities and experiences. Those experiences lead to . . . do you see how this works? Learning about pipes has also taught me about history, culture, and art. All of these things sharpen a mind that is ripe for ideas.

Truth be told, I don't consider myself an expert in *any* area. Not being an expert used to bother me. It doesn't any longer. I'm happy that I know a little about a lot of things. The Idea

Mentalist is always curious, always asking questions, always seeking the experts and sitting at their feet in hopes of learning something new. And, it's fun. When I talk about "playing the expert," I don't mean you should lie about being one. I mean, be playful in your pursuit of knowledge.

Nearly twenty years ago, my friend introduced me to single malt scotch. I was at Ted's beautiful home, saw his scotch collection, and I was fascinated. I asked him to pour me a scotch and tell me everything he knew. Ted poured me what I now know as a "finger" of scotch in a beautiful glass. The glass had a small stem and resembled a tulip—slightly flared at the rim of the glass. I now know the glass was specifically designed to flaunt the bouquet of the scotch as well as keep my hand from warming the scotch as I held it.

I buried my nose inside the glass immediately and breathed deep like I would a glass of wine. I now know that one shouldn't do that with a scotch in order to protect your olfactory nerve. I also now know that a good scotch glass is designed to allow the scent of the scotch to waft as you pass it by your nose, to give you the best experience.

I took a big gulp of the scotch that Ted handed me. It had a very peaty, smoky, and unpleasant taste to me. I thought I had swallowed Campho-Phenique. I now know that the scotch he handed me is meant to be sipped, not gulped. I also now know it was not really an intro-level scotch and Ted was tricking me. Some scotch requires a bit of getting familiar with. I have now developed a taste for that scotch, and I respect it.

I asked Ted if I should add ice to it, and he smiled politely and shook his head. I now know that the way I drink my Tennessee Whiskey (spelled with an E-Y) is a much different experience than drinking Scotch Whisky (spelled with only a Y). And, while you can do whatever you want with your scotch, aficionados generally frown upon ice. They also have strong opinions about whisky stones and the amount of water (untreated water, that is) that can be added to change a scotch's chemistry and awaken other flavors, etc.

For the next five years, after my first scotch experience, I read over twenty books about scotch. I tasted every scotch I could get my hands on. And, yes, I started collecting scotch glasses (my poor wife).

I soon found myself hosting scotch tastings in my home. In my basement. By candlelight. I started a group in my home called Aqua Vitae (water of life). Each of the participants were invited as if it were a top-secret society. The wax-sealed envelopes arrived at their homes requesting that they pledge never to reveal our secrets (I had to have a few conversations with wives to assure them nothing weird was happening since their husbands said they swore an oath and couldn't tell them what was happening).

Each of the twelve participants contributed 200 dollars a quarter so we could pool our resources and afford scotches we wouldn't buy on our own. We drank together, learned together, had new scotch experiences together, laughed together, and deepened our friendships. Ted was part of that group, and he would often make jokes about the Young Padawan becoming the Jedi.

One day, a friend heard about Aqua Vitae and asked me to teach a class on scotch. Soon, I was doing this more regularly. When another friend told me how he had to raise money for a non-profit he was starting, the Idea Mentalist in me suggested a scotch tasting fundraiser that worked like a mini-Aqua Vitae. Before I knew it, the fundraiser was sold out and we had raised thousands of dollars for his project.

Am I a scotch expert? Not by any stretch of the imagination. But, if you compare me to that inquisitive young man almost twenty years ago, I seem like an expert to many.

My scotch experience rhymes with so many experiences I've had over the years that started with a curiosity and led me down a road of learning that opened my mind to new ideas. I dare you to pick something and work on becoming an expert.

A Play Smorgasbord

I could write forever about making play. I could keep telling stories. But, I'll wrap it up with a few brief descriptions of things to try on for size and you can develop your own stories.

Rename your staff meetings: In one of my past work experiences, meetings had become a drag. When I arrived on the scene, I renamed our staff meeting "Sandbox." Everyone got a pail and shovel on their desk with an invitation to our first Sandbox. We never used the term, "staff meeting" again. The Sandbox was a place where we playfully gathered to get on the same page.

Walk in the rain: Everything looks different, smells different, and feels different in the rain. Watch how people act and react in the rain. Stand under shelters you've never stood beneath. Walk around with a cup of coffee from your favorite local coffeehouse and see how you experience life differently.

Take a camping work trip: This works best if you have a camper, but it's not the only way to play. Grab your camping gear and find a campground that's close to you. When they are close, you typically wouldn't stay there on a normal vacation. Do all your phone calls and computer work beneath the canopy of trees while a campfire burns. See what happens to the way you think.

Play "What if?": Sit by yourself or with a special friend. Go old-school and grab a pen and paper (or, get daring and buy yourself a brand new journal just for this play time). Write "What If?" at the top of the page. Begin to make a list of things you might never think of doing or things that aren't in the hopper.

What if we sold everything and moved for fun?
What if I bought a sports car?
What if we ate vegan for a month?
What if we didn't watch television for a year?
What if we started collecting mugs?
What if we visited a new bakery every month?

Discuss your lists and try some things on for size. Just because.

Binge-watch TV shows you wouldn't normally watch: Not a fan of vampires? I dare you to binge-watch a vampire show. Not an avid documentary watcher? I dare you to watch a documentary on something that doesn't interest you.

Cook like Chopped: Have you ever seen *Chopped*? In this television show, four chefs compete in three rounds where they make dishes with unusual ingredients. Their dishes are then judged. Have someone go to your refrigerator and pull out random ingredients for you. Make something yummy.

Repaint: Repaint your living space. Just because. Pick a color you've never used.

Stay in a boutique hotel: Just for fun, book a room in a boutique hotel near you or in another city. The amenities won't be the same as a big, posh hotel. The rooms will be older and smaller. Take in the details. Imagine what it would be like to live there.

Take on a web alias: Sign up for a Twitter account anonymously. Pick a fun name. Connect it to a new Gmail account. Start tweeting things you've never tweeted out of fear. Be funny. Ask new questions. Make bold statements. Don't do it to make people angry or stir up a fight. Do it to interact in new ways and hear from different people.

Switch your day off: For years, I took off Mondays because my weekends were super busy at work (I only had one day off. You might actually have two). One year, we decided Friday would be fun instead. We did different things on Fridays than we would have on Mondays. Fridays were alive in our town, and Mondays were dead. We stayed out later. We laughed more. We experienced different things. Soon, Saturdays felt like the beginning of a new, refreshed, exciting work week. I had way more energy. I thought differently. What day might work better for you?

Take naps. Sleep in. Go to bed late: Whatever your normal routine is for sleep, try changing it up. See if your activities change. See if you think and create differently. See if your attitude changes.

Wear wigs and masks: I have a friend who playfully keeps costume wigs and masks in his car at all times. You never know when you might need one to create laughs. Wear one to the office party. Wear one to the staff meeting. Wear one on your daily walk.

Ten Great Things: Gratitude can be the antidote to so many things. Boredom. Despondency. Complacency. Mediocrity. Anger. All of these things rent your head space when it could be full of ideas. Start a list of Ten Great Things that happen to you every day. Post it on Facebook or some other social media outlet. Invite conversation.

CHAPTER EIGHT
INNOVATION TRAINING

I don't run. I'm fond of saying, "I run when there's danger." I've had friends invite me to go jogging, enter 5ks, do marathons, and a bunch of other things I put in a category labeled "Why?" I don't understand running.

However, I'm astute enough to know that if I were to want to run a marathon, I would need to start training. I'd need to keep eating right and perhaps augment my diet. I'd need to build up my lung capacity. I'd have to stop some habits. I'd have to get used to stretching.

Training would require me to . . .

Stop some things.
Start some things.
Continue some things.

Being an Idea Mentalist is like being a runner.

Innovation takes training. My friends who are big-time competitive runners see the world differently than those who don't run. They scope out trails. They think about BMI. They wear Fitbits. They chose different restaurants. They read books and magazines that I wouldn't pick up in a million years. They try out new workout routines.

To innovate as an Idea Mentalist, you need to start to see the world differently.

In this chapter, I hope to give you a few exercises to stretch your idea muscles. The more we stretch these muscles, the more frequent our ideas begin to surface and take shape.

Stare-Stepping

No need to call out a typo. S-T-A-R-E Stepping is a practice of looking at an object for an extended period of time and coming up with a list of uses for that object other than the original intended use.

Stare-Stepping is one of my favorite group interactive experiences for teams. The activity is fun, and it opens the door for the "it doesn't have to work this way" conversation. It also can bring everyone's personalities, convictions, fears, and insecurities to light.

One of the most memorable team Stare-Stepping activities I hosted was with a group of about ten people in a California company. We sat in the round, and I placed a five-gallon, empty, clear water jug in the middle of them. The team had to answer a question with one restriction. The question was, "What is this?" The restriction was that no one could answer that the item was a water jug.

I gave these two simple rules and left the room.

What happened next was what typically happens in an organization where people don't feel permission to speak, disagree, or innovate. Everyone froze (except for Tina, who we will meet in a bit).

I sat outside the room listening in on the conversation.

"Are we just supposed to have one answer or many?"
"Do we write it down?"
"Is it a metaphor?"
"Is this a trick?"
"This is stupid."
"Come on, you guys. This is fun." (Tina, by the way.)

I came back into the room to give a bit more instruction and speak to the fear and the issues that were surfacing the questions. I gave them permission to think freely and write their answers down with the promise of no ridicule or chastisement.

After fifteen minutes, I returned to the room. "Who's ready to share their answers?"

Richard (the names have been changed to protect the innocent) went first. "I still don't know the point of this, but I'm going to say it's something to keep coins in." I thanked Richard for playing even though he wasn't a fan.

Andrew went next. "I don't really like being put under pressure for these kinds of things. I like to process and have time to think. But I also think it could be a piggy bank." Then he paused and looked like he was painfully mustering up the courage to say something else. "I also think it could be a seat if you turned it on its side and filled it with something."

I applauded in approval. "Great job, Andrew. Anything else?" Andrew shook his head.

Then, Richard mumbled something under his breath. I asked him to speak up. He did. At the volume of eleven, in an angry tone. "This is stupid. We don't make things out of water bottles here. And you didn't tell us to write down multiple answers. This meeting is a waste of my time. Who made you the creativity judge? You think you have some corner on the market?"

Richard was correct. I never said to write multiple answers. I also didn't say to write down one single answer and leave it at that.

In almost every group I've done this exercise with, there is a Richard in the room. For one reason or another, Richard rejects the idea of innovation. Richard likes the status quo. Richard feels threatened by anyone who might threaten the way he enjoys working. If you want to be an Idea Mentalist, you cannot be a Richard.

Karla spoke up next. "I think it's a water bottle. That's what it was designed for. People are always trying to change things or make them better, but I think some things are great the way they are, and we should celebrate that. Why do we always have to change things?" Thanks, Karla. You have a right to your opinion.

Tina went next. "Well, I have a whole list of things." Eyes rolled in the room. I think Richard's eyes actually made a sound as they rolled. Apparently, Tina always had a list of ideas. No one was surprised. The group had become quite used to mocking Tina for her long lists. I was thrilled to hear her list.

A planter.
A drum.
A lampshade.
A suggestion box.
An instrument.
A toy for playing keep-away.
An ashtray.
A vase.
A windchime.
A picture frame.
A bird feeder.
A birdhouse.
A cat food container.
A grease trap.
A worm bed.
A basket.
A bath toy for her grandson . . .

Tina went on and on. All in all, she had around fifty things on her list.

Over the next couple of days, I got to know Richard and Tina (and the whole team) a lot more.

There are many differences between Richard and Tina.

Richard is afraid. Tina is not.
Richard doesn't like change. Tina thrives with change.
Richard wants to keep his job because it is his identity. Tina realizes that who she is is not what she does.
Richard has become lazy and just wants to finish his career with as little conflict as possible. Tina wants to finish strong in everything she does and, quite frankly, she doesn't really think about life in terms of finishing.
Richard is mean. Tina is kind.
Richard is selfish and will never be an Idea Mentalist unless he undergoes open-heart surgery of the spiritual kind. Tina has a strong character and a desire to help others.

Tina was a joy to be around. She possesses and embraces within her spirit both freedom and permission—essential items for the Idea Mentalist. Tina asks the question, "Who says it's not a bath toy?"

Try Stare-Stepping for yourself. Pick another random object in your home or at work and make a list. Take note of the feelings you have as you explore ideas. Try doing it in a group. Look for the Richards and Tinas. Make mental notes of what you are repelled by and what you admire.

Stretch those muscles.

Reshape Group Brainstorming

When I talked about becoming a runner, I mentioned there would have to be some bad habits I'd have to stop. In this chapter, we'll talk about things to start, things to continue, and some things to lay aside.

In my opinion, contrary to popular belief, brainstorming is one of the worst things an organization can do for generating ideas. Or, at least, the typical brainstorming meetings I have observed in my lifetime—and there have been countless many.

In a typical brainstorming meeting, the meeting is usually not announced in advance and brainstorming is a spontaneous response to a problem that arises during the meeting.

In the brainstorming meetings I've observed, there are usually one or two loud voices that dominate the conversation, and they aren't necessarily the most helpful in the room. Or, if they are helpful, everyone else feels like they cannot do any better than the A+ student.

Most brainstorming meetings I've seen rehash the same old ideas over and over and often nothing gets done. There is no action plan. Or, if there is, something is settled upon rather than wholeheartedly embraced.

Brainstorming meetings often make people feel frustrated because they are ill-prepared, feel put on the spot, are afraid to disagree, and resurface the frustrations they felt from the last brainstorming meeting where nothing got done.

In my opinion, the best group idea-generating comes when:

- people have enough time to prepare
- everyone is required to bring at least one idea to the table (I suggest one to three ideas, but you can set the outside parameters however you want)
- action plans are given at the end of the meeting

If you have the power to steer what happens in your company meetings, try idea generation in this new way. If you don't have the power, consider suggesting this to your boss or person in charge.

Buyer beware. If you try this new way of group idea generation, you are going to have haters. If you require your staff/workers/team to bring ideas to the table, the *Richards* of the world are going to show up swinging.

Fine. Let them swing. And . . . don't invite them to the next idea meeting.

One Midwest group I worked with tried this new way of idea generation on for size under my guidance. The time of day, the rules of engagement, and the expectations were clearly laid out. Most people were looking forward to gathering.

As expected, the *Richard* in the group protested. He came to the first meeting ready to fight.

There we sat in a room at the time we all agreed upon. There were designer donuts and craft coffee on the table. There was an expectancy in the air that overpowered the fear and intimidation that could also be felt. Some people were laughing. Some were just quiet. There was a wipe-off board on one wall. Everyone was there ready to play, except for . . . Richard (a different Richard this time, but another version of the same guy).

Richard strolled in ten minutes late. He didn't apologize. To make a long story short, Richard was angry that he was "required" to do anything. He was angry that he was a manager and was not consulted on the time the other manager set for the meeting. He was angry that the process was being changed. Richard also . . . *did not* bring an idea.

There was another protester in the group that day. Her name was Liza. Liza ran an important wing of the company, but wasn't known for her creativity. She was known for her ability to run a "well-oiled machine," as the saying goes. Liza also showed up to the gathering without an idea. She wasn't angry like Richard, but she did make it known that she preferred to "observe and respond."

The first meeting with this group was mildly productive as everyone shared their ideas. We spent most of our time getting to know one another. At the end of the meeting, I announced there would be another idea-generating meeting coming up, with the same rules as this one.

I put the meeting on the calendar with the main person in charge and sent out the invitations. I did not invite Richard or Liza.

As you can imagine, they were pissed. When people made their way to the second meeting the next day, Richard asked, "Where are you headed?" People told him what was up. Richard stomped into the room where I was sitting and told me I needed to invite him. "I'm one of the #*^%!ng managers here!" he said.

"Yes, you are Richard. But, you made it clear you don't want to be part of this idea generation on these terms. However, your boss has decided this is the future. One idea was your ticket to the show. You knew what time we started and passive-aggressively showed your disdain by showing up late with an attitude. Just because you're a manager does not mean you have the right to buck the system and not participate."

And Richard resigned.

Now, before you feel sorry for Richard and say something like, "I can see Richard's point. Not everyone is an idea person," let me say you are right. I can see his point too. But, his point is wrong. He wasn't asked to be an idea person. He didn't even need to have a great idea. He needed to have *one*. And, he needed to be a team player.

To expand upon the running metaphor, imagine your team is in a relay race. Everyone needs to train together. If someone refuses to grab the baton, pass the baton, set their own course, or shows up wearing a flannel and jeans to run in, you have a problem.

Richard could have shown up on time with a half-baked idea and calmly told the team, "This was hard for me. I don't really like coming up with ideas." And that would have been okay. We could have asked Richard if he wanted to excuse himself from the next gathering. We could have asked Richard if he was willing to stretch and learn to become an idea person. We could have asked Richard if he wanted to meet one-on-one and talk through his fears.

Part of successful group idea generation is gathering the people who actually want to talk about ideas. Don't weigh your organization and possibilities down with the Richards of the world who poo-poo everything that is not on their terms.

The wrong people with the wrong attitudes will keep you and your team from good ideas.

Learn to Recast

Metal workers know what it means to recast. Recasting is the process of melting down metal objects and reshaping them into something else.

Directors know what it means to recast. Recasting is the process of finding a new actor to better tell the story you are trying to tell on the stage or in film.

Book editors and college professors know what it means to recast. Recasting is the reorganization of thoughts to better capture what it is a writer is trying to say.

Idea Mentalists know how to recast. Recasting is the ability to see an idea for what it's worth and reshape that idea for a new context.

Once upon a time a high-profile church in the Midwest, in a wealthy neighborhood that embraced the arts, decided to do something no other church was doing. They started writing dramas for their weekend gatherings that would present a situation, tell a story, surface a need to listen, present a conflict, etc.

The church was very influential, and soon churches all over the world started emulating what this church had done. They thought, "If it's working for that church, surely it will works in ours."

One church in Portland, Oregon, admired the midwestern church and decided it would also write its own dramas. So, week after week, month after month, for years on end, a team would meet to talk about the weekly message, music, and what the crux of the drama would be. A small but decently talented drama team would memorize these scripts each week.

After a few years, the drama director sat down with the leadership team, exhausted. Sad. She came to tell them she was resigning. She admitted it was extremely difficult to write meaningful dramas so readily (they also borrowed scripts from other sources at this point in the game, but still wrote a ton themselves). She also admitted that her drama team was waning from the pressure, and it was increasingly hard to recruit and keep people around. She spent way too many nights working. She never got a weekend off.

The sad thing is, most of the people on the leadership team had their hunches that this wasn't working years before they got to this point. But no one said anything.

Even sadder . . . a growing percentage of the congregation thought drama had run its course years before, and the sketches had even become kitschy and juvenile to some. Many thought that drama should never have been a part of what was happening in this Portland church.

No one ever stopped to ask before they pulled the trigger, "Is drama right for *us*?" Truth be told, it never really was right for them. The congregation was very close to two seminaries and a Bible college. Most of the congregants were overworked and stressed-out students and intellectuals who much preferred discourse to theater. They weren't fuddy-duddies by any means, but they weren't necessarily the drama crowd.

Had someone done a good job of dissecting what made drama a brilliant idea in the Chicago area, they would have stumbled on some amazing ways of thinking and come up with a good list of questions that may have helped them innovate in ways that worked for them in Portland. They could have *recast* the idea of drama for their culture.

Whenever you are stretching your idea muscles in hopes of recasting, ask yourself these questions:

What do I like about this idea?
Is there anything like this in my context?
What is it about my context that rings true with this idea?
Has this idea been tried before?
What exactly is my context (where do I live and who are my people)?
What am I selling with this idea?
Would this idea work as-is in my context?
Can I appeal to wisdom regarding this idea and vet it with any trusted confidants?
Am I willing to work towards Version Four?
Do I believe in this idea enough to explain it as if it were my own?

Do I believe in this idea enough to be able to cast a compelling vision for it?
In light of what I know, is the idea worth recasting?

The church in Portland that fell in love with the idea of drama eventually closed its doors altogether. It's a sad story. I imagine they could have done so many innovative things to help their community had they asked the right questions.

Coincidentally, another church I know had a similar experience with drama. However, they *did* ask the right questions—not from the beginning (which would have been ideal), but shortly after they jumped into the deep end and realized they were going to sink. I had the privilege of spending time with them as they asked the questions and came up with good answers. It went something like this . . .

What do we like about this idea?
There seems to be a growing arts community in our town and drama is part of the arts scene.

Is there anything like this in our context?
Not really. Not right now.

What is it about our context that rings true with this idea?
A growing art scene in our town.

Has this idea been tried before?
Actually, yes. A few times. It didn't work. Even the local city theater group struggles every year to get participants and people to pay for shows.

What exactly is our context (where do I live and who are my people)?
We are a midwestern town with struggling auto workers who have been displaced. We have a lot of welders, upholsterers, steel mill workers, auto painters, and other blue-collar workers

in our town. We also have a big agriculture community and quite a few vineyards in the area.

What are we selling with this idea?
We want to tell old stories in fresh ways. We want to capture people's attention. We want to create conversation. We don't want church to be boring and we don't want the experience to be dry. We have compelling stories.

Would this idea work as-is in our context?
No. Not really. We tried.

Can we appeal to wisdom regarding this idea and vet it with any trusted confidants?
Yes. Let's put together a team of people who have the same vision for our church and town.

Are we willing to work towards Version Four?
Yes. Let's do something different and make sure it's right for us.

Do we believe in this idea enough to explain it as if it were my own?
Not drama. No way. We aren't willing to bleed for it.

Do I believe in this idea enough to be able to cast a compelling vision for it?
Not drama. But, we are excited to do something different. Fresh. Exciting.

In light of what we know, is the idea worth recasting?
Yes. Let's get to the spirit of the idea.

To make a long story short, the church embarked upon an incredible journey over the next decade. Their journey of recasting started with asking the right questions. Their answers led to more questions and answers. They became one of the biggest benefactors to their town. They became known throughout the community as a group of people who actually cared for other humans. They breathed life, time, money, and energy into their arts community, in their town that was way more of a music town and a visual art town than a theater town.

They did a fine job with their weekend gatherings and infused them with new music that was written by local artists. They started a visual arts team that exploded on the scene and attracted a number of artists that felt like they finally had a place to call home. Their teaching was the talk of the town— compelling and interesting. Their focus on telling good stories through art surfaced the writers in their midst and many began self-publishing books. They hosted music festivals that supported up-and-coming singer-songwriters. I could go on and on.

To this day, they continue to innovate and ask the right contextual questions. Asking the right questions is why their former senior pastor, my friend David, recently bought a run-down Victorian-style home in the area and turned it into a training center for other pastors who want to innovate in their context. His center includes a recording studio, wood shop, metal shop, writing lab, regular guest speakers, and plenty of space to create. Not your grandfather's church project.

I know a leader of a company who is swayed by every single new idea that someone else is doing. He is always on the lookout to save his company and, quite frankly, make himself look good. He has tried numerous ideas over the years for marketing, product placement, and new product lines. He has even hired numerous people with the hopes of having *them* find a new idea that might save his company. But, his company flails year after year with a lukewarm response. He's also made a lot of enemies along the way. His organization could be influential if he would just ask the right questions.

I know a businessman who changed the vibe, vision, and decor of his shop many times. Almost every time he traveled and was captivated by another shop in the same industry, he changed *his* shop. He spent thousands upon thousands in hopes of finding what worked in his town. He had at least three major conversations with his staff where he cast a new vision for a strategy and vibe. He lost everything. I'm convinced he would still be in business if he had asked the above questions.

When you see a good idea in another context, ask the right questions before you bet the farm on it. Identify what you love about the idea. Recast it.

Write Down All the Ideas

I sat in an idea meeting where everyone was asked to come prepared with at least one idea. There were fourteen people in the idea meeting (a bit large, if you ask me). There was a wipe-off board at the front of the room and the person leading the meeting was writing down ideas as they were presented. Kinda.

Everyone's ideas were being summarized on the board until about the fourth person presented. The moderator acknowledged the idea with nods and smiles but didn't write it down. He moved on to the next idea.

I didn't say anything at first. I thought it was a mistake. Perhaps he forgot. Perhaps he didn't really know how to summarize the idea. I had grace for this *oversight*. I vowed in my head to remind him of the idea before the meeting was over.

However, a few ideas later the same thing happened.

So I stopped him.

"Why didn't you write down that idea?" I asked.

He replied, "Because we've done something like it before. It's not a new idea."

I then asked, "Why did you not write down the idea from earlier?"

He replied, "I didn't really think it would work for us."

I carefully instructed the group (without trying to shame the moderator) that *every* idea should be written down in an idea meeting. Even if it's been done before. Even if someone doesn't like it.

Don't expect people to follow you in the future if you ignore their contribution.
The person with the idea may not know it's been done before.
Value every person by valuing every idea.
The person with the idea may have a slant to the idea that is worthwhile.
The idea may lead to another idea.

Writing down every idea is also a good rule if you are generating ideas on your own. There have been many times throughout the years where I've gone back through notebooks of scribbled ideas and landed upon a goldmine that either was overlooked at one time or passed on for some reason. Because of this, I make it a habit to go through old notebooks once a year.

Ask, "What Does My Community Need?"

I'm surprised how many of us don't innately ask this question when we are dreaming of new innovations. We touched on this a bit earlier. "Great Ideas are Indigenous" is Tenet Thirteen. Indigenous ideas are ideas that make sense with who you are and where you live—be that local, regional, or global.

Asking what your community needs is a good filter to run ideas through. It's also a great exercise to take some time and ponder the question to set yourself up for thoughtful idea generation.

Spend some time in the space that inspires you, or the space where you can be uninterrupted with a pad and paper. On one side of the paper, write down a list of things that identify your town or city.

You might write down the low-hanging fruit like *nature trails, sports programs, community events,* and *water sports*—things that are highly visible and obvious. Dig a bit deeper into the headspace of your town when you make your list. What is important to your town? How do people in your town generally think?

You might write things like . . .

. . . *family-focused*
. . . *environmentally conscious*
. . . *health and fitness addicted*
. . . *school pride*

If you dig further, you might paint with large brushstrokes and make calls like . . .

. . . *overworked*
. . . *money-motivated*
. . . *upwardly mobile*

You might make observations about your town being very multi-cultural or having a lack of diversity.

On the other side of your list, start writing down what you think your town lacks, needs, desires, complains about, dreams about, etc.

You might write things like . . .

. . . need for diversity
. . . opportunities for artists
. . . cheaper entertainment for families
. . . better transportation
. . . live music
. . . more mom-and-pop restaurants
. . . downtown parking

A fun and often fruitful exercise is to then take this list and draw lines between your observations.

What happens if I cross *family-focused* with *opportunities for artists*?
What are the implications of my *health and fitness addicted community* needing *cheaper entertainment for families*?
If my community is *overworked*, what does *cheap entertainment* look like?

Ideas are often about connecting dots between needs, desires, and gaps in the space where you live or the grander economy.

Paint

I used to work with a short-sighted leader who thought highly of himself and often spoke in leadership platitudes. One of his favorites was, "We should never change for the sake of change." It was one of the things I constantly disagreed with him about—even when he tried to explain. He warned of the dangers of cataclysmic change, unplanned change, and hasty change. Of course, there is some validity to his fear-of-change in a variety of scenarios, but he believed the statement so deeply and was so afraid of change that he *never wanted to change*. Every potential change was vetted, processed, and committee-ed to death. Really. To death. As in, ideas would die.

Idea Mentalists create change just because. And, in so doing, they condition the people around them to see change as inevitable and normal. They may even begin to see change as welcome.

One of the easiest ways an aspiring Idea Mentalist can condition themselves (and those around them) for change is cheap (relatively speaking), easy, and accessible. It's as quick as a trip to your neighborhood paint store.

Start looking at the walls around you as canvases. Look at them as spaces to try on new moods. Don't like the new color as much as you thought you would? Change it again.

New paint says, "change is welcome," and "nothing is permanent." Paint says, "I am not afraid to try new things."

New paint also inspires other changes, like wall hangings, pillows, rugs, and throw blankets. That's also how ideas work. One small idea can inspire a whole slew of rhyming ideas.

Go Beyond Paint

What could happen if you looked at walls not only as canvases, but as innovation surfaces? What if those surfaces were more than just something that held up a roof, but something you interacted with on a daily basis?

One of the coolest projects I was ever involved with gave me permission to use the walls of multiple rooms in interactive ways. I was given carte blanche to design a learning environment in multiple rooms where children would learn lessons through various teaching styles incorporating story/drama, science, art, music, digital technology, and general kinesthetic interaction.

In these environments, walls created more real estate to engage with. Walls didn't exist to simply hang something on.

Vertical surfaces were lined with chalk paint, cork board, hanging rolls of colored butcher paper, pipes where students could talk at one end and listen on the other, musical instruments, cabinet doors that opened to writing surfaces, touchscreen computers, video gaming systems, magnetic surfaces, dry-erase surfaces, a Buddha-Board surface, a green screen for filming, a wardrobe closet, painted tarps used as theatrical backdrops, and a living wall with plants that needed nurturing. Students would be introduced to a lesson multiple times over the weeks and months and engage with the topic from different perspectives and tactile methods. And, they still had all the conventional tools filling the room to use as well—tables, computers, art supplies, books, and audio equipment.

One of the greatest things about using all the vertical surfaces was they never looked the same. They were a rotating canvas of magnetic word poetry, student art, digital photos, dramatic scenes, scribbled notes, essays, and diagrams.

These rooms worked so well that the management team decided to create the same kind of environment . . . in the office space. For the adults.

Capturing and fostering innovation has been relegated to what we write down with pen and paper in most environments that exist in the world. Change it.

Repurpose

The Detroit "eye sore" formerly known as the Cadillac Stamping Factory was originally built in 1925 for the Hudson Motor Company. General Motors purchased the assembly plant in 1956 and made bumpers, hoods, and fenders for Cadillacs there for over thirty years. It remained mostly vacant since the 1980s, with minor operations from another company until about 2015. In recent years, it was announced the building would be demolished to make way for a brand-new 684,000 sq. ft. industrial building that is expected to create 450 new jobs for people in automotive and manufacturing careers.

Hold that thought.

Enter Wallace Detroit Guitars, "The Sound of the City."

In 2014, Mark Wallace started a company that, in my mind, is one of the most innovative repurposing companies in existence. Wallace's company builds guitars from the reclaimed wood of Detroit buildings that are being destroyed and builds beautiful guitars with the soul and bones of Detroit history.

I saw an article about this company a few years ago and fell in love with the concept and the beautiful pieces of art Wallace is making—no guitar is alike. Wallace is making history from history. He's an artist and an innovator. Not only do they look beautiful, they sound amazing.

I love what their website says . . .

Detroit has always been about music.

And it's always been about making things.

Smokey Robinson. Jack White. Iggy.

The Model T. The Mustang. The Coupe de Ville.

They all have the same things in common: the vision to break all the rules in pursuit of something new—and the discipline to make whatever we make with obsessive attention to detail.

That is the attitude of an Idea Mentalist if I ever heard one. On December 22, 2016, two adult "elves" showed up at the place I worked. They told me they had a package from Santa. They unrolled a scroll and read a poem about me. I started to cry. They pushed a large box across the floor and told me Santa said to open it right away. Inside, I found a hard brown leather guitar case. I opened the case to see a Telecaster-shaped, butterscotch-colored electric guitar made by Wallace Detroit Guitars out of wood reclaimed from the flooring of the old Cadillac Stamping factory. More tears. Snotty tears.

Every time I play that beauty, I relive the story. I retell the story often.

If not for Wallace, what would have become of that wood? That reclamation and repurposing changed my life and made for an amazing story.

Not every flowerpot that's turned into a lamp is going to change a life. Not every horseshoe turned coat hook is going to prompt tears. But, the act of repurposing not only teaches us about art and frugality, it teaches us to think differently. Repurposing creates a new story.

Recycle Materials for New Projects

When I was in charge of all the visual art and design of a church in Michigan, we would have people come from all over the world to see our building. The building itself had an incredible design and purpose, and the eye candy inside was never stagnate, always collaborative, and sure to create conversation.

Often, people would visit the space and I would hear them say things like, "I wish we could do something like this, but we don't have the budget." I would always chuckle and tell them a story about the budget I had to work with. They were always blown away at how little money we spent to make art, projects, and beautify our space. Sometimes, the budget was $0.

We built a team that was not afraid to ask for help, not afraid to ask for things for free, and not afraid to recycle materials we had used in another installation or aesthetic.

One time, my friend Joel—who has drawn comics for Marvel—created illustrations for a story we had written. We enlarged those drawings and glued them to 4 x 8 foam core panels. Those panels hung throughout the space, so it looked like you had walked into a graphic novel. Creative lighting made it come alive.

When people saw the installation, they swore they could never afford something so creative. But, it was only foam core, paper, and some glue. The foam core had been used in countless other projects over the years. They had been painted on, glued on, stapled on, varnished, and carved into numerous times. The initial investment may have been $400-500, but we recycled the foam core over and over and over. And, to be honest, the foam core was donated from a contractor who had leftovers from a big job.

My wife and I have a deal about t-shirts. If I get a new one, I have to throw out an old one. Easier said than done. My t-shirts are stories (you're probably sensing a pattern here). My t-shirts are from concerts, friends' bands, events I've volunteered at, National Parks we've visited, and gifts that have been given me. I have a lot of t-shirts.

For a while, my wife allowed me to keep a bin under the bed of the lesser-worn shirts and I would rotate them. But once upon a time, they were getting too much even for me.

I was telling my friend Dianne about the shirts. She was always playfully teasing me about my quirks and celebrating them at the same time. She's one of the most encouraging people ever. "Give me the shirts," she said. "Don't throw them away. I'll make them into a blanket for you."

Soon after, Dianne quilted for me my favorite blanket ever. Many memories have been preserved in that cozy blanket. The shirts were recycled and repurposed.

Dianne took what I had (old shirts bound for the trash) and combined them with what she had (quilting experience). A t-shirt blanket might not seem earth-shattering at all. It's not supposed to be. But, the more often we think like Dianne, the better we become at being an Idea Mentalist. And, who knows what other ideas might be sparked for Dianne or me because of that blanket?

Recycling materials teaches the aspiring Idea Mentalist to work with what they have and think differently. You don't always have to invest more to get more. You may already have your investment. Just dream of how you can use it differently.

Create Experiences: Themed Restaurant House Parties

My mother-in-law always had the best Christmas Eve dinner parties when I was dating her daughter and for a few years following our wedding. She turned conventional Christmas meal expectations on their head for me. When I would go to Jack and Lynda's on Christmas Eve as a young man, I wouldn't expect to eat grandma's old cornbread recipe, or a cranberry sauce recipe passed down through generations. I didn't expect to find a dry turkey on the table or expect to smell stuffing in the air.

Instead, I anticipated the printed menu at each place at the table where our creative original name placards were found. The menu was sometimes a shocker for a 17-year-old. Frog legs. Escargot. Venison pâté. Gazpacho. Vichyssoise. Quail.

Duck eggs. The list goes on. It wasn't always super crazy, but unconventional for sure.

Lynda has always been a queen of creating experiences.

Lynda's playfulness was passed on to her daughter, Tahni, my wife. And, it now shows up in different ways, like the entire family making sushi for Thanksgiving. Or Tahni's penchant for making a meal we've never had simply because she wants to. Or, in one of my favorite ways, like when Tahni throws a dinner party themed like a kind of restaurant.

One of my most memorable themed dinners was in the mid-2000s, when Tahni invited my whole team over for dinner in our basement. We had a huge basement in the Midwest—bigger than our first home. Tahni turned the entire place into an Italian restaurant and served a four-course meal. If you didn't know it was my home, you would swear you were in Italy. The music. The smells. The decor. The cuisine.

We learned a lot about my team that night because, in this atmosphere, they talked differently. They told stories of vacations. Stories of their favorite meals. Stories of their family traditions. We grew closer and fostered trust in this environment. This faux Italian restaurant in my basement grew our team in ways that made it easier to dream about the future and ideate together.

On a personal level, practices like this help the aspiring Idea Mentalist to break from ruts such as the "what do you want for dinner" rut, where we gravitate toward the same five things we rotate through. They help us create habits of designing engaging experiences. Never underestimate how these tiny adventures shape the mind of the Idea Mentalist. Don't put them in the category of frivolous activity, or say, "I just don't have the time." Idea Mentalists MAKE TIME for innovation training.

Do Your Day Backwards

Currently, a "typical" Monday for me includes a supply run for our restaurant that includes at least four different stops at various suppliers, a stop by our warehouse, unloading all the items I've procured, answering emails, confirming weekly appointments, and various social media designs and posts. Sometimes, my granddaughter will come along for the ride if she doesn't have school.

My supply runs might begin with the furthest store from me (about forty minutes away), and I work my way back to the shop. I stop and get lunch on the way back. I unload the supplies then come home to do the paperwork and computer stuff. This order of business often works well with the timing of some suppliers' will call windows. It also allows me to be back in town for appointments that can only happen in the early afternoon.

When I do the day backward, it's an entirely different Monday. When I start with the suppliers that are close to me, I don't leave the house as early. I enjoy a cup of coffee while doing the computer stuff. Sometimes I have appointments with people in town who can only meet in the early morning. I end up eating at a different place for lunch. I can ask my daughter if she wants to go with me and I pick her up after I do the local runs and the kids are in school. I meet different people working different shifts in the stores. The ciabatta rolls and baguettes I need from the bakery are handed to me hot from the oven and make my truck smell wonderful.

Doing a typical day bottom-to-top from a usual routine is a great exercise for innovation training, if for no other reason than staying out of ruts and creating new experiences.

Job Shadow a Friend

You've heard of Take Your Child to Work Day, but you've probably never participated in Job Shadow Your Friend Day. Because, I made it up.

On several occasions throughout the years, I have asked my friends if I could job shadow them. Work their shift with them. Tag along. Learn their world.

I've gone to work with beer brewers, winemakers, restaurateurs, coffee roasters, ER doctors, radio DJs, auto mechanics, and engineers for large computer companies, to name a few.

Not only have I learned a ton about my friends and created pathways to understand them better, but I've also experienced other worlds that have cross-pollinated with my world.

Who knew that the day I spent with a brewer would lead to me designing a brewery? Who knew that my day with a winemaker would lead to me making a charity wine and raising thousands of dollars for an art school? Who knew that a day with the coffee roaster would help me better understand exactly what I was looking for years later when I opened a coffee shop? Who knew that working with DJs would rekindle my love for radio and I'd start writing jingles again and doing regular radio appearances?

Create Moments that Foster Community

Some time around 2005, I was trying to breathe life into the arts community in our city as part of my new job, but I didn't know many visual artists or musicians because I was new to the area.

There was an old building in our midwestern town that housed a hodgepodge of struggling businesses and vacant spooky-looking spaces. I loved the vibe of the building though it needed some TLC. Some artists lived in the building and would occasionally sell their creations there out of loosely defined stores.

Michigan is a lot different than California, and, at that time, artists were living and working in the space that suffered from bad insulation, up-to-code electricity, and lacked sales permits. It was probably illegal on many levels, but no one in any position of power or authority was wasting time or money to slap down fines or ultimatums. Imagine a bunch of 1960s-era love children showed up on a bus one day and decided to create their oil canvases, pottery, metal sculptures, and birdhouses in a commune-like setting in a dilapidated building and you'd be close to imagining what it was like at this building.

I called the owner of the building and asked if I could have permission to camp there for a few nights with my buddy, David. All we needed was space. He obliged and we brought our sleeping bags, a coffee pot, a Frisbee, guitars, an amplifier, and an SLR camera.

On night one, we sat outside on the covered porch of the old brick building and played guitar. Birdhouse Guy came and sat with us as he played drums on his knees. Then, other artists joined in. Harmonica Player guy showed up. Someone else grabbed another guitar. I kept playing and my buddy started tossing the Frisbee around with another artist. Dancer Girl began twirling things and dancing in the parking lot. Someone started tossing paint on a canvas. We took long-exposure photos of playing games and dancing in the moonlight.

In the morning, we made coffee for everyone. It was appreciated after the long, late night of play. For another whole day, we created together and swapped stories. They loved hearing my vision for the arts in the town and they were hungry for someone to help surface a need in the area to pay attention to them and what they had to offer. At the time, the city had no idea they had a wealth of musicians and artists that really wanted to breathe hope into the city. The city needed them, and the artists needed someone to help lead.

That couple of days would change the trajectory of the arts in my corner of the world. Over the next few years, the artist community began to thrive. The artists, including myself, began to collaborate in amazing ways. Live music that had all but disappeared in the city became a treasure once again.

Do I think that those two days in that building were "the" catalyst for change? Not exclusively. Do I take all the credit for changing the arts scene in the town? Absolutely not. Do I believe that something happened over those two days, coupled with a wave of other events and experiences that completely changed the face of the arts in that city and how the city interacted with artists? A resounding yes! The next decade would boast one of the most vibrant periods of time for the arts in our city for as long as anyone could remember.

About eight years after the commune campout, a group of artists would return to that very building—now under new ownership, renovated, up to code, and full of various legit businesses like a theater, a salon, multiple art galleries, a coffee shop, a metal shop, and an arts academy that specializes in helping children who were being neglected. The artists created art over a 24-hour period in a live event that was open to the public for twenty-four hours straight as well as being streamed online. People placed bids on art in real time, and thousands of dollars were raised for a local charity. As we created throughout the night, some of us told stories of that night on the porch of the building so many years earlier.

This event was called ARTapart and was repeated in other years. It was one of many events that were launched in part because like-minded people began to hang out together and foster community in creative ways.

Back up to 2005 . . .

Always Form and Value Relationships

I didn't know it then that night on the porch at the spooky building, but the biggest problem in Jackson, Michigan, was not a lack of opportunities for artists. It was not that the city didn't really care about art. It was not that there was a lack of vision for the arts. All of those were true to some degree, but they weren't the biggest issues. All of those issues could have disappeared and there still would have been a huge problem with the arts in Jackson. The issue was relationship. Or, lack of relationship.

Everybody likes to be part of something special. Everyone wants to be noticed. Everyone wants to be known and to know someone cares for them. Thankfully, these are the beautiful things that happen when relationships are cultivated, nurtured, and cared for.

The Idea Mentalist must understand that, in order for their ideas to begin to surface, in order for their ideas to ever come to fruition, in order for them to thrive as an idea machine, they must be committed to relationship. Sure, an idea sneaks through every once in a while, and it comes to fruition because of one person's hard work and creativity. But, Lone Ranger Idea Mentalists do not experience longevity. We need each other.

The single most important thing that happened that night in 2005 was that a community began to grow. Out of that community and the community that grew over the next few years, some of the most creative ideas I've ever seen infused life and energy into a town that had a very poor self image. When relationships are cultivated, the soil is ready for ideas.

However, the Idea Mentalist does not look at people as commodities. This is very important. We cannot see people as simply a means to our ends. We don't form relationships because people can provide something for us. However, we do understand that when we do need another person's help with that special thing only they can provide, it works best when the relationship has been a priority with no strings attached.

I love helping people. But, I know all too well what it feels like to be used. I know what it feels like to be contacted by someone who acts like we are best friends because they need something from me. My friend calls these people askholes. I never want to be an askhole. Neither do you.

The Idea Mentalist puts a priority on relationships because people are worth it. One of the benefits of prioritizing people is that we build a history and trust. And, when we need each other, we are willing to help because we know we are loved just because and not because of what we can offer.

Frank is known in his community as a "good leader." He's not. He leads a big company that, on the outside, looks thriving and healthy. Inside, there is a sickness. Frank is good at surrounding himself with people who get things done and have good ideas. They make Frank look good. But, Frank has a long history of shallow flattery that gives people enough energy to perform for a season, then get hurt and frustrated because they don't feel valued or heard in the long haul. Frank comes on like a friend and dismisses people like clearing the cache on his computer. When Frank senses their frustration, it's usually about the time he figures he's done with them, and he cuts them loose. There are so many bodies buried under Frank's business he should be called an undertaker.

Let's be frank. Let's not be Frank.

There are a few test questions an Idea Mentalist can ask of themselves to make sure they aren't being a Frank.

Do I invite people over to my home or out on the town to spend time with them?
Do I respond to others' invites to spend time with them?
Do I get my hands dirty helping others?
Am I someone that people would feel free to ask a favor of?
Do I celebrate others publicly?
Do I give people credit for the things they have helped me with?

Practice Helping Others Surface Their Ideas

I've already mentioned that an Idea Mentalist expects to meet new people all the time. We must expect to have daily conversations with people. An Idea Mentalist's innovation training habits must include interaction with other people.

One of the things that has become second nature to me at this point is asking good questions about people when I'm talking with them. An Idea Mentalist must care about people, and we exercise that care muscle by being interested in others. One of the best ways to show interest is to ask questions and spend time listening to the answers.

One of the most satisfying things for an Idea Mentalist is not only mining their own ideas but helping to surface the ideas of others. This only happens in meaningful conversation and sometimes multiple conversations over a long period of time. And, might I add, it should happen with the permission of others. I'm not saying that people are our projects and we should always suggest ideas to them. That would be annoying.

I've believed for a long time that everyday, ordinary people have the wherewithal to do incredibly creative and unique things if they believe in themselves, someone else believes in them, and they are given license to tease out their ideas. Sometimes, Idea Mentalists help others arrive at these places by playing the role of *guide* or *coach*.

Dan (not his real name) is an auto mechanic. He used to fix my cars. Dan has that "I'm just a normal Joe and nothing special" attitude. He's incredibly humble, helpful, and kind. But, Dan doesn't believe he is anything other than a good mechanic. Or, at least, he used to think that.

Dan always makes jokes about himself. He has a very self-deprecating humor that borders on self-abuse at times. If you told Dan he could change the world, he would make some joke about barely being able to change a spark plug.

I think Dan is an amazing individual. I've seen him work his wizardry in the garage. I've seen him make deals on non-operational automobiles and fix them up to turn a profit. I've seen him donate his time to help others who can't afford him.

I used to look forward to taking my car to Dan. It took him a couple of hours to fix my car, but another couple of hours just to chat, tell jokes, and talk about life.

In one of these conversations, I was telling Dan about an art and music project I was part of that was raising money for charity. Dan said something to me like, "You always have some amazing idea like that. I just keep fixing cars and hoping something great will happen one day."

Dan kept going on and on about how he was going to die with a wrench in his hand without really having made a difference. I asked Dan for permission to tease some things out with him. I asked these questions:

What is something you do that people need?
What group of people needs what you offer more than anyone?
Do you know any other people who do what you do that might
be interested in partnering to do something special?
Are you willing to take a risk and work hard to make a
difference?

Dan answered these questions enthusiastically. Here were his answers:

What is something you do that people need?
I fix automobiles. I do regular maintenance like oil changes.

What group of people needs what you offer more than anyone?
Single moms and low-income families need extra help.

Do you know any other people who do what you do that might
be interested in partnering to do something special?
Absolutely. I know a ton of mechanics and garage owners.

Are you willing to take a risk and work hard to make a
difference?
When do we start? And . . . what are we doing?

In the next five minutes or so, Dan and I imagined pulling multiple people together who did auto maintenance and owned garages to provide a free service to single mothers on one weekend in multiple locations. Then, we got to work contacting everyone who might be able to help. We reached out to sponsors, the radio station, garages, mechanics, groups that provided services to single moms, churches, shelters, and a number of other grass roots businesses and influencers.

Sponsors provided thousands of dollars to purchase barrels of oil, advertising, food, and auto parts. Over a weekend, multiple garages and mechanics provided FREE oil changes to hundreds of single moms. While they were waiting for their oil change, they were fed and given resources for extra help. An organization was present at multiple sites to provide education about child seat safety. Face painters and balloon sculptors entertained children. Hundreds of hot dogs and hamburgers were given away.

With each oil change, a safety inspection was done on vehicles. If something was found to be dangerous, a group of people onsite decided if there was enough money to fix it and then approved the parts and labor for immediate care or a future appointment. Moms were surprised that weekend with fixed faulty brake lines, new tires, and new brake pads. All for free.

Part of an Idea Mentalist's innovation training will include looking beyond their own desire to create ideas and redirect their energy to helping others discover their potential.

Dan had an idea. He just didn't know it. The event became one of the most celebrated events in his city that year. Hundreds of single moms were surprised and blessed by generosity.

All because of a simple mechanic who had "nothing to offer," and an Idea Mentalist helping him understand he was lying to himself.

Be an Interest Chaser

Idea Mentalists are inquisitive. Constant learners. They have an insatiable hunger to learn about things. They are obsessed with researching those things they want to know more about. They lean into these unquenchable urges to learn more, and they make time and room in their lives to gain new knowledge.

When I was designing a brewery/restaurant in Michigan I met a man named Eddie. Eddie is very talented. He is an airbrush artist and a welder. He knows construction. He used to customize automobiles and motorcycles. He's funny, spunky, raw.

My friend Heidi and I were working on the mural in the brewery when Eddie came on the scene. We were creating a timeline of the history of beer on a huge wall with creative steampunk-rich images. In fact, the entire brewery now has a steampunk theme, complete with funky lamps made of old steel auto parts and gears, instruments that have been adorned with pipes and gauges, oil canvases of top hats and corsets, and our gigantic mural. I've been a steampunk enthusiast for a while, and it was fun to work out my creativity in the public space as opposed to just making cool costume jewelry and funky steampunk weapons in my garage. Nerd alert.

I'll never forget the day Eddie came up to me and asked if he could help. He told me he was a great airbrush artist and could really enhance our images with shadows and cool color fades. What makes the moment so memorable is the question Eddie asked me when we invited him to join us. "What is steampunk?" Eddie asked.

What makes his question so shocking and memorable is that Eddie would go on to be a contestant on the first season of the Game Show Network's reality television show, *Steampunk'd,* in 2015. Ten designers of various mediums competed in steampunk-themed challenges for the chance of winning $100,000. Spoiler alert: Eddie won.

Before Eddie took home the cash, wrote a book about his experience, taught art classes to children, donated a ton of art supplies, and became a hometown hero, he chased down his steampunk interest with the passion of a child in a game of playground chase.

Eddie would create art every night after he'd get home from working on the brewery. Each time, he'd send me photos, asking, "Is this steampunk?" I remember my answers. "That's cool, but just spooky. Not steampunk." "That's macabre, but not steampunk." "That looks very Tim Burton, but not steampunk." Eddie continued to craft and eventually found his steampunk rhythm.

As soon as he grasped the concept, he began creating free-standing art with me for the brewery. He was a better welder than me, so we did it in his garage. One of my favorite pieces was a large floor lamp made with cogs, gears, copper tubing, steam gauges, and a giant Edison bulb. We crafted it with a giant steel spring so the lamp could sway.

It wasn't long after that Eddie told me he had been contacted by the Game Show Network because of some art pieces he had in a show. Even though it had been a short period of time since he asked me the question, "What is steampunk?" to ending up at the television studio, Eddie had invested hundreds of hours in the world of steampunk. He had developed super fun ideas about how to construct steampunk art with moving parts. His imagination was running wild with ideas about steampunk jewelry, furniture, and costumery.

When Eddie went to Los Angeles to film, we were so excited for him. When he came back to town after filming, he couldn't tell us a thing about his experience because he had signed a non-disclosure agreement. We would all have to wait for the show to air to know the outcome.

Between filming and the air date, our family moved back to California. We would watch the show on the West Coast, and I would message Eddie after the episodes. On the final night, when Eddie won the grand prize, my wife and I jumped off our sofa screaming and dancing. I called him in tears to tell him I was proud of him. He told me he owed it all to me.

But, he *didn't* owe it all to me. I just happened to be the guy who was there when he started a journey of discovery and relentless pursuit of something he is passionate about. He did the hard work. He did the innovation training.

What question do you need to ask today? What are you chasing down? The Idea Mentalist is always running after something.

CHAPTER NINE
A WHOLE NEW WORLD. OR . . . A WORLD RESET.

In the summer of 2019, my wife and I began having vision-casting parties in our backyard to generate excitement about our dream business we were going to be opening. Anticipation was in the air. We remember these gatherings as being quite magical. We cooked up samples of the food we would offer and served fun drinks that would become a staple at our new place. A plethora of inventive ideas were shared at each gathering.

The parties were extra special because our home was filled with people we care about. We had an extra sense of how special that was because I had just lost a job that severed relationships and carried deep pain. I was still licking very fresh wounds as people celebrated in my backyard and it eased the pain and helped me focus on what really matters to me.

Every guest at our parties was handed a twenty-five-page business plan for our new adventure that we named *Reset: Café by Day*. The first page gave a feedforward short description that was worded in present tense—as if we were already open.

> **Reset** is first and foremost in the *experience* business. We are a local business committed to good service, an interactive aesthetic, community engagement through events and education opportunities, live music and entertainment, being as environmentally friendly as possible, and giving back to the community as a financial benefactor.
>
> Our food and drink revenue streams are coffee, tea, beer, wine, pastries, and small plates of food. Other revenue streams include but are not limited to a VIP/ Conference Room, catering, a monthly subscription box, and personalized coffee and tea blends. Merchandise streams include branded merchandise, events, consulting, education events, and mug clubs. Our revenue streams provide us the opportunity to

do what we really love in life—creating engaging experiences that are ripe for *community* interaction.

***Experience* and *community*. This is what we offer.**

The tagline, *A Café by Day,* hints that we are something different at night—which we are. While we maintain a café feel throughout the day, we transform our space every early evening into a night-time venue with a different food and drink menu, different lighting, different music, different uniforms, entertainment suitable for an evening crowd, and an entirely different mood and vibe. Whether day or night, we are committed to an environment that is:

Stylish and uniquely distinctive Imaginative and inventive Community focused and responsible Interactive and participatory

These are our Strongholds—the things that make us exceptional. They are the sieve through which we put every potential decision and the standard by which we measure our success.

The rest of the business plan is fun and gets into market research, funding, specific revenue expectations, and all the things you would expect for a detailed business plan.

The most important part of the whole plan is found in the first two paragraphs.

***Experience* and *community*. This is what we offer.**

Not only were we stirring excitement for this new cafe and giving our friends a snapshot, but we were also generating interest in our Founders Club that would help generate cash for us to move forward. We had a local potter handcraft one hundred numbered Founders Mugs. Over the course of a few months, we sold one hundred Founders Lifetime Memberships. Founders get discounts on everything at Reset, and they are able to take their mug down off our shelf whenever they visit to fill with their favorite hot or cold beverage. The Founders Club is a community within the community—a group of people we feel close to. Of all the things we offer at Reset, the Founders Club is our most obvious example of *experience* and *community*.

We got the keys to our new building in November of 2019, and immediately started the renovation. Many friends helped in the deconstruction on a few weekends. We tore out four 700 lb. Romanesque columns. We ripped out adornments that had been attached to the walls as if they were meant to withstand an earthquake. Old facades, tapestries, shelving, and signage were removed. We built and upholstered benches on either side of the space. New paint throughout. New glass in the entire front of the building replaced the old etched glass that sported grape leaves. We installed new equipment in the kitchen and back rooms and a beautiful espresso machine that I jokingly (not jokingly) told people was worth more than our barely used Toyota 4Runner. We bought and made furniture.

Before we opened, we encountered way more expenditures than anticipated as we retrofitted the electricity and plumbing. The health department told us we could not use a lot of the equipment we purchased from the old wine bar. The Health Department also found some issues that had been missed or overlooked with the last tenants, and asked us to do additional upgrades to bring everything up to code. Our dollars were majorly stretched, but we had hope as we counted down to opening day.

We hired our staff and began training in February of 2020. We flew to Seattle to learn how to operate and maintain the new espresso machine. We secured all our vendors. We began advertising and sponsoring. We did everything you'd expect a new business owner to do and more. Exhausted yet hopeful, we set a grand opening date. March 9, 2020.

Throughout February, we would hear stories of something called a "novel coronavirus," but it seemed like a distant and non-threatening illness. Santa Clara County was the first California county to declare a local health emergency, but it was a blip on the radar. There was news of quarantines for travelers from Wuhan, China, at Travis Air Force Base in Fairfield, California, but it seemed very contained and not likely to affect us. In mid-February, news of over 700 people being infected on a cruise ship had more prominent coverage on the news, but still seemed like something that was happening "over there" away from us.

Late February would bring reports of multiple conferences being cancelled over concerns for the spread of the virus and the first talks about California's economy starting to be affected made the news. As cases began to multiply and counties continued to declare states of emergency, talks of "what will happen with our schools" were the order of the day. More local emergencies, more deaths, more uncertainty.

On February 29, Reset had a private party for our Founders. Live music, food, and lots of beer and wine were flowing. Our forty-five-person capacity venue was full of smiling faces, laughter, and expectation for a prosperous future.

By the first week of March, the world had an expanded vocabulary. *N95 masks, COVID-19, coronavirus, isolation, containment,* and *quarantine* were used in everyday conversation. On March 6, the President signed an $8.3 billion dollar relief bill that was promised to aid in the development of a vaccine, improve treatment, secure health equipment, and provide money for small businesses and state and local governments.

On March 2, Reset: Café by Day did a soft-open. We didn't tell a soul except our Founders. We simply opened the door and waited for people to stumble in as our staff practiced making coffee, food, and cocktails. We pushed heavy on social media for a March 9 Grand Opening.

On March 7, San Francisco introduced a new term as they banned all "non-essential" gatherings in facilities that were city-owned. *Essential* and *non-essential* were added to our daily vocabulary. On that same day, Elk Grove Unified School District became the first school district to shut down in California.

On March 9, Reset opened with great fanfare.

On March 11, the WHO declared COVID-19 a pandemic.

On March 12, Disneyland closed its park in Anaheim and most major league sports postponed their seasons. The State and Federal tax deadlines were extended.

On March 13, President Trump declared a national emergency, which put more money into the relief pipeline. More schools closed. Restaurants were asked to reduce seating and practice *social distancing* (add a new term to the vocabulary).

On March 15, Gavin Newsom, the governor of California, ordered the complete closure of all bars, wineries, and nightclubs.

On that same day, Reset had its first staff gathering. We started with praise for our staff and made special mentions of those who were going above and beyond. At the end of the meeting, I told my staff, through tears, that I had no idea what the future held and no idea when I'd be able to schedule them again. We told them there would be no hard feelings if they looked for another job.

On March 16, I sat at home in the evening wondering what was going to happen next. I heard President Trump tell everyone to stay away from restaurants and Newsom tell restaurants to do takeout only. I poured a scotch.

The rest of the timeline is painful. But, this should suffice to surface something very important. Reset was built on *experience* and *community*. These were the very things COVID-19 threatened for us. It's also worth mentioning we had already gone without an income for eleven months as we tapped our savings, expecting we would soon have cash flow.

What does the Idea Mentalist do *when the world shuts down and experience, by definition, necessitates practical contact with things and each other?*

What do you do *when the very community you are hoping to bolster and augment is ordered to stay home?*

What do you do *when all of your amazing ideas have been mandated into non-existence?*

What do you do *when all your side hustles that generate income are also non-options because they require you to be in close contact with people?*

What do you do *when those other revenue streams are fineable offenses, and no one would hire you anyway since businesses and individuals are leaning into risk-averse behavior, over exploration in a time of stress?*

COVID-19 was not our first bad news rodeo. I'm assuming it wasn't/isn't yours either. Bad news, suffering, loss, hardship . . .

nobody wants them. They always suck. And, they always have the power to break us . . . or make us.

Take a moment. Ask yourself what your suffering has taught you. I'm not asking you to celebrate your suffering. That's ridiculous. I'm not asking you to turn that frown upside down. That would be insensitive. I'm asking you to ponder what you've learned over the years as you pass through the suck. Here are some things we learned about navigating hard times by going through hard times:

- **lean in to Intuition**
- **let go of the specifics and focus on the mission**
- **focus on people**
- **focus on your community**
- **focus on the things that spread joy**
- **remember we have each other and that's enough**

Lean In to Intuition

I strongly believe everything I discussed in the first part of this book such as "A Commitment to Version Four" and "Incubating Ideas." But somewhere along the line, you may find you have no time, no security blanket, and a crisis to work through. It's then that knowing there's an OPTION C and "Believing You're Creative" kick into high gears.

It's in these moments that *intuition* is your greatest ally.

Intuition can scare people. If you are in a corporate setting and you press hard for your idea to be adopted based on your "gut feel" or your "hunch," you may get a lot of pushback—unless your hunches have proven successful many times and you have a track record. Outsiders who don't experience your personal intuition may call you names like "flighty" and say you like to "shoot from the hip." *PS, these people usually don't have ideas and stay stagnant in their fear.* Intuition isn't provable. The only way you prove your intuition is trustworthy is when your idea works. Even then, the naysayers may say you got lucky. We use intuition all the time. We make choices every single day based on what we believe is right for us and others. Little expressions of intuition may be something like making a decision to drive a different way home because something feels "off," or going out of your way to encourage someone because you sense they need it. I made a deal with God years ago that, whenever someone randomly pops into my mind that I haven't thought about for a while, I give them a call and check on them. I'm always amazed at how often people ask, "How did you know?" Sometimes, intuition feels like magic.

There isn't a more magical example of intuition than that of *mother's intuition*. It's an otherworldly thing. Mothers are connected to their children in a way that no one else is. There are countless stories (maybe in your own life) of mothers knowing when their child is in need, knowing when they are in trouble, knowing when they are missing, knowing when they are hurt, knowing where they have run off to, and knowing "what they did." This is that *sixth-sense* intuition.

Much of intuition can also be seeped in life experiences and tools we've been sharpening for a long time. When the intuitive moment hits us, we may not be able to say exactly *why* we know it's right, but many things may have been playing into our intuition for years.

The ability to listen well.
Seeking wise counsel.
Life experience.
Things we've seen.
Stories of others.
Being a student of nature.
Having a teachable spirit.
Trying and failing and succeeding over and over.

In the HBO hit series, *Succession*, Logan Roy's children always talk of their father as having great intuition about the family's media empire. It makes them uncomfortable. They wish they had it. They want it enough to lie and cheat and manipulate for it. They hate that he has it and they don't, so they joke about it and call him names like "God." But, even though Logan Roy is a horrible person, he has decades of experience that play into his intuition, as opposed to the power-hungry, greedy, mean-spirited, and entitled children he raised.

Sometimes intuition is felt in the gut. In the chest. Some experience hot flashes. Others experience actual visions.

Intuition is real.

It doesn't mean when you act on your intuition you will *always* be right. But, you can't ignore it. You will always learn from it. It is always telling you something.

Let Go of the Specifics and Focus on Mission

Mission may be an outdated and overused term that the business world has all but ruined for me, but we all know what it means. It's that thing you must do, or you are not who you say you are. It's that mountain you die on.

Everything we planned for Reset revenue streams were threatened. Classes. Live music. Parties. Special Events. On and on and on. Those were not the mission; they were the specifics.

True confessions. I'll admit that when I get married to an idea, it's often hard to let it go. But COVID-19 didn't come with a plethora of choices. I'm also very committed to an aesthetic and style and *vibe* that blows minds, and I have very quirky necessities that people don't often understand. Before COVID-19, I said:

"We will never use paper napkins."
"We will absolutely not use plastic utensils."
"We refuse to put signage all over our shop."
"We won't sacrifice our menu."
"We will never do takeout."

COVID-19 pointed its crooked devil finger at me and laughed.

We immediately cut our wonderful menu back to flatbreads, baked goods, whole bean coffee, and bottles of wine.

We immediately started stocking up on paper goods, boxes, and plastic utensils.

We made all the regulatory signs that were required of us.

We immediately came up with a takeout plan and invested in to-go boxes.

In a perfect world, the details and specifics that set you apart matter. In a world-turned-cesspool, your mission matters. Period.

An Idea Mentalist knows that sticking to mission will pay off. Somehow. Someday. People will notice. People will feel it. People will talk about it.

NOTE: *This doesn't mean let go of ALL the details. Just ask yourself what really matters in the long run and if your sacrifice can be reversed or altered one day.*

Focus on People

When we gathered in our backyard for our vision-casting parties, someone asked me if we would ever do takeout. I remember clearly saying, "We will never do takeout."

Yet, on March 16, my wife and I began to brainstorm all the ways we could make takeout happen without a staff—just the two of us. I never wanted to do takeout because of the presentation limitations. The packaging looks cheap, and you can't control what happens to the food when it leaves your establishment. Will it roll around in their car? Will it be cold by the time they get home? Takeout is not the *experience* or the *community* we were looking for.

I heard a story once about Paul Stanley of the band KISS talking with his recording engineer. I hope the story is true, but I can't prove it. The engineer said that what they recorded sounded awful. Stanley told him to fix it. The engineer told Stanley, "You can't polish a turd." Stanley replied, "No. But you can paint it silver."

Takeout seemed very turdy to me. We didn't start a business to offer flatbreads in a paper box and cocktails in a plastic cup with a closed lid. But, let's face it . . . COVID-19 and all its fallout is one big turd.

Tahni and I talked over options and asked all the questions we knew to ask as Idea Mentalists.

We knew we did not want the two of us to be at the restaurant all day long just hoping someone would come down and order something—especially with a stay-at-home mandate in place and restaurants being held hostage on what they could actually offer.

For instance, takeout cocktails were permissible as a temporary emergency order in March, which allowed restaurants and bars to sell to-go cocktails, beer, and wine, but the catch was you *had* to serve it with food. This would confuse people for months on end as some establishments were eventually granted permission to sell wine and beer without food, but restaurants still had to sell alcohol with food. Not any food, mind you.

There was a whole list of "not permissible" food items on the ABC site. Many bars and restaurants chose to give the finger to the rules all over town and sell to-go booze with a cookie or a bag of chips (or no food at all)—confusing the issues even more.

Every day, for months after we finally did our first re-open, our staff would be brought to tears as someone yelled at them and told them they didn't know what they were talking about. We got accused of lies and manipulation for keeping to the rules.

So, what was our silver paint? The silver paint was "a new kind of *community* and *experience*" that allowed us to foster relationships even with the crippling regulations. It wasn't what we hoped for, but when we started asking questions we came up with some amazing ideas.

When we put the focus on the people, the ideas we generated were better. The more we focused on people, the more we were able to swallow the daunting regulations and restrictions. The more we focused on people, the more energy we were able to salvage.

We asked, "What does our community need?"

They need to still feel connected to something bigger than their quarantined home.
They need help celebrating even when they are in the suck.
They need something to look forward to.
They need to feel cared for.
They need a personal touch.

So . . .

We turned our lives into a reality tv show of sorts. We started a weekly online conversation about wine from our backyard where Tahni and I could goof around with each other and talk about our wine special that week. We paired our wines with the special flatbread that week. The live chat experience made us feel connected to our people and them to us.

Winesdays became a thing that folks looked forward to. They would place their orders each week and pick them up on Winesday Wednesday. Every week we looked forward to the line of folks outside of Reset on a Wednesday waiting to pick up their goods at a distance while we delivered with masks and gloves. We made so many new friends during this time. Doing all our takeout on one day of the week with a ridiculously simplified menu gave us all something to look forward to.

We started Take-and-Bake specials for holidays and special occasions. Some of these specials included personal delivery from us to their doorstep—not from DoorDash. From us. On numerous occasions we logged over 300 miles a day. Christmas. Easter. Mother's Day. We delivered bags of coffee door-to-door. We delivered scones and mimosa packages. We delivered cookies.

To see smiling faces from a distance as we left food and coffee was priceless. To get letters from moms about their mimosa packages made us smile. To see multiple pics of people online enjoying their fresh ground coffee as they reset from home gave us a daily drive to keep going.

We created ways to stay in touch with our community in the digital world. If they couldn't come to us, we were coming to them. Besides our weekly livestreams, I started a weekly Zoom interview with politicians, business owners, artists, educators, local government officials, and people who are doing great things in our community. Reset Coffee Convos aired over 50 interviews on our Facebook page weekly beginning in early 2020. The feedback from our community about how helpful the conversations are is outstanding.

We celebrated people who are doing amazing things in our community with giveaways, discounts, and specials. On Teacher Appreciation Week, we asked students to submit stories about their teachers and why they should get a gift certificate to Reset, and we awarded teachers with gift cards. We told their stories online.

Focus on Your Community

Even after the total shutdown of restaurants, and the steps that occurred approaching a total reopen, COVID-19 would threaten to kill us. Outside seating, 25% indoor seating, and 50% indoor seating all carried with them a bit of false hope. No restaurant was built to survive on 25% or 50% seating.

While outside seating and limited indoor seating stopped some of the bleeding, it also came with a price tag. Sure, you could be outside, but it was cold and sometimes raining. We bought propane patio heaters, and some kind people donated some more heaters to us, but propane cost us $1,000 a month the first fall and winter. Oftentimes, we'd see homeless people come by and just turn on the heaters to stay warm, and we'd have a small moral dilemma. It was also a dilemma when someone would order one cup of coffee and sit outside for an hour by themselves under a heater burning away every bit of revenue that coffee provided. When limited seating opened up, we were also required to provide hand sanitizer and barriers, at additional cost

But, we had to keep painting the turd.

We took steps to draw attention to other businesses as well as ours. We knew we weren't the only ones experiencing hardship in our city.

We ordered takeout from other businesses and left five-star Yelp and Google reviews for them. *PS, if it wasn't a five-star experience, we didn't leave a review. We refuse to leave bad reviews online in the space where people wield the power to shame one star at a time.*

We joined forces with the bookstore across the street and added a message on the bottom of our receipts offering a 10% discount at Ruby's Books for that day if they brought their Reset receipt. Ruby's Books added the same message to their receipt offering customers a 10% same-day discount at Reset.

We teamed up with our local chocolate shop, Snook's, and started selling boxes of chocolate that were made with Snook's chocolate and Reset's single-origin Brazilian roast coffee. Cross-pollination for businesses is a beautiful thing.

Focus on the Things That Spread Joy

My wife and I used to have discussions once upon a time about what would happen if I ever lost my job. We never thought it would happen, but it's always good to be prepared. We always felt secure that we both have well-rounded experiences to rely upon.

Then I really lost my job and soon after . . . COVID-19.

Every one of my side hustles and well-rounded experiences required that I travel and be around people. But, the one that really killed me was not playing music for a crowd. All the regular music gigs I had that were helping put food on the table dried up overnight between losing my job and COVID-19. Music gigs for festivals, weddings, private parties, restaurants and bars, birthday surprises, street parties, church gatherings, even funerals, for crying out loud. All gone.

We worked to keep music alive against all odds. Here's the thing about music . . . If I don't play it or hear it, I curl up and die. Many feel the same. Just because I wasn't able to play in coffeehouses, wine bars, and on stages didn't mean music had to stop—especially because folks still wanted to hear it.

We hosted our own online concerts live from Reset and our living room.

We did an all-request online concert where people emailed me their song requests the week prior and I played them all, complete with dedications.

We hosted online concerts with multiple artists and streamed a coordinated event, recorded in the homes of multiple musicians, in order to raise money for music education.

When outside seating was granted to us, I began playing every single Sunday morning outside of Reset on the street. We named it The Sunday Reset. Positive music. Positive vibes. Every Sunday. When it was cold outside, I played. I played with a firepit in front of me. I played under cover in the rain. Sometimes I interjected some encouraging stories. What I thought would be an experiment for a couple of months has lasted almost two years at the time I'm writing this.

One Sunday morning, it was about forty-five degrees outside. I lit my propane bonfire pit and pulled it close to me. No one was on the street. I started at my normal start time of 9:00 a.m. I played a set of about five songs for me, the occasional passerby, God, the angels, my ancestors, the universe, the birds and squirrels, the feral cats, and the pets attached to humans. Then, one person showed up and sat at a table by herself with her coffee. A few filtered in around her over time, but not many on this cold morning.

Plenty of other Sundays by that point had had much more traffic. Bicyclists stopping for coffee and pastries. Runners. Pet owners with their fur babies. But, this one forty-five-degree morning sticks out to me like no other. Because, this one woman sat by herself with a cup of coffee for an hour and thirty minutes. Listening. Crying.

At the end, she came up to me and said, "This community is exactly what I needed. You guys are the real deal. There is something special about this place."

The words still ring in my head. "This *community* . . ."

We teamed up with local videographers and photographers to tell stories of hope and humanity. My friend Bill owns a business called Portlight Creative and he's committed to telling compelling stories. He's especially attracted to stories about people making a difference. My friend Jacob is a professional photographer who operates the online entity known as Folsom Eats. He tells great stories about food by capturing shots that make you want to lick your computer or phone screen. He also has a heart for the stories that are changing our local world.

All of us joined forces to tell multiple stories over many months about good things that were happening in our city and in our Historic District where Reset is located. We posted these stories online in multiple places. We all want to hear good stories. Especially when the mainstream media is sharing mostly bad ones. Idea Mentalists know "Creativity Flows from the Positive."

We sponsored a poetry contest for local schools. One of my greatest joys is being on the board of the Wildwood Performing Arts Foundation (WPAF). The Foundation is committed to music education and gives opportunities to students and up-and-coming young artists to learn our rich American musical heritage, immerse themselves in music, and have a platform to perform and hone their craft. The Foundation needed a good idea to help keep up community interest and maintain involvement with students in a world in shutdown.

Enter Project Heart Beat. Project Heart Beat is a poetry contest run through local schools with the guidance of the Wildwood Performing Arts Foundation. Students write poems based on pre-selected themes and submit them to their school. Winning poems are then given to WPAF and we gather a group of professional musicians to turn winning poems into songs. We perform the songs in a concert setting and record them for the students to have forever. Winning poets are also awarded musical instruments, lessons, concert tickets, and various gift cards from local businesses.

For months in the thick of the pandemic, we worked on Project Heart Beat with the hope of being able to perform a live concert in an outdoor setting without the lockdown restrictions in place at the time the project was birthed. In the summer of 2021, we experienced the fruit of our lockdown labor when we performed the first Project Heart Beat Concert with students and parents in the Historic District of Folsom. There are few things in life more precious to me than performing a song I wrote in collaboration with an elementary school student poet. To watch their face light up as they hear a band play their song for the very first time is a magical thing.

Remember We Have Each Other and That's Enough

Not only did COVID-19 threaten to destroy our revenue, but our costs also increased. Dramatically. In the first six months we had over $25,000 in unforeseen expenditures.

Our refrigerators went out and needed repairs.
Our oven needed to be replaced.
Our air conditioner died.
We needed to purchase a new ice machine.
We needed patio heaters for outside dining in the cold.
We needed misters for outside dining in the heat.

Yada, yada, yada.

The COVID-19 railroad continued to lay new tracks through our dreams at every turn, with every new regulation, with every new expenditure, with every new restriction.

One morning, while looking closely at our financial situation, I asked my wife if we could talk about something that I thought might upset her, but I felt like we needed to discuss. I had an idea I wasn't sure she would like.

My wife and I have always found that setting up the hard discussions with a disclosure like that at the forefront helps medicine go down easier and helps us decide when it might be the right time to talk so we both have a clear head. Tahni said it was a good time to chat right then.

The idea I had was a problem-solving idea. Remember our definition of an idea from the very beginning of this book: "An idea is a *new* thought introduced to the present situation as a proposal for a course of action." I can guarantee you my idea had not been entertained up to this point.

At our kitchen table, in our beautiful Historic District bungalow that my wife had turned into an urban cottage of fairytale proportions, I said, "I think we should sell the house."

Sometimes, the Idea Mentalist will come up with an idea or set of ideas that only work with a long-game mentality. The idea will hurt in the short run. The idea may save one dream and crush another in the short run.

For the next few minutes, we talked math-talk and made a list of all the things we could do if we pulled the money out of our home in a seller's market. Not only did we talk about what could happen if we sold the house, we talked about a world where we sold . . . everything. Everything we didn't absolutely *need*.

What if we sold . . .

   . . . *the house*
   . . . *the cars*
   . . . *the furniture*
   . . . *the travel trailer*
   . . . *the art*
   . . . *the keepsakes*
   . . . *the patio furniture*
   . . . *the tools*

And, what if we could generate enough to . . .

   . . . *pay off some business debt*
   . . . *pay cash for a bigger trailer*
   . . . *pay cash for a smarter car*
   . . . *pay cash for a truck to pull the bigger trailer*

And, what if we . . .

   . . . *lived full-time in our trailer*
   . . . *lived debt free*
   . . . *bought ourselves some more time to try and make the restaurant work*

So that's what we did.

The Idea Mentalist is prepared to act on ideas that have the power to move you or someone or something forward. Propel you up and out. And sometimes, buy you time.

Have you ever been in an uncertain transition period? Where you don't know what the last chapter looks like? But, you sense you're in the middle somewhere? It's a state of **liminality**. Liminality is the space between. We all experience it in one form or another.

In the liminal state, it's good to have something to look forward to, for sure. But, it's even more important to know what makes your soul content.

For my wife and I, our contentment is with each other. We are okay saying we will be content with each other in a trailer with two dogs, trying to save a restaurant and a dream. We are content to say, if Reset ever crashes and burns, we will high five each other and say, "Good game." Because, COVID-19 is evil. And, we know we have worked and we *are working* the ideas. Hard.

No matter what happens, we will never say we failed.

And, we will not fail each other.

CHAPTER TEN
WHERE DO WE GO FROM HERE?

We've been on quite a journey, but it's not the end. It may be the last chapter of the book, but we've got a long way to go. There are ideas to be spoken into existence.

I heard Willie Nelson once say something like, "Songs are easy to write. There are melodies floating in the air. You just have to reach up and grab one." Part of what Willie said is poetic. Hyperbolic, maybe. It's a word picture. And, part of what he said is very true for Willie. Willie can pull melodies out of the air. He's credited as having written over 300 songs—and those are the published ones. No one is counting the ones he threw away, abandoned, gave away, or the ones sitting in a notebook somewhere to be found fifty years after he's dead that will be recorded on a tribute album. Songs are easier for Willie because he's done the time. He's an Idea Mentalist.

There are ideas floating in the air.

In this final chapter, I'd like to mention some of the people and groups that have helped me harness those ideas that are floating around. They've helped me test the ideas. Shape the ideas. And, some have even worked alongside me to bring the ideas to fruition.

Life Editors

I've mentioned this a few times in passing now. Four times now, to be exact. But, I want to go deeper here and stress how important I think this is.

This is worth mentioning . . . I grew up in a religious culture that talked a lot about accountability and accountability partners. These were the people that would make sure you were doing the things you committed to do and to not do. They were a type of volunteer religious police who you asked to scold you when you were wrong. They were the people that helped you accept responsibility. In my experience, accountability partners seldom made me feel good about myself. For any of you that had or still have that as part of your experience, *a Life Editor is not an accountability partner*.

A Life Editor is someone who will . . .

- call you on your BS because they know you well enough to recognize the lies you tell yourself
- help you grow through conversation and experience in order for you to become the best possible version of yourself
- help you not be what you may be unhealthily compelled to be
- encourage you and lift you up
- be a good sounding board

A Life Editor is someone . . .

- you love and trust
- who doesn't have a financial gain at stake in your health or wellness or ability to perform
- you've invited to give you feedback and critique
- who is honest
- who listens well
- who has wisdom/insight/intuition/life experience
- who loves you for you with all your quirks and brokenness and beauty and gifting

A Life Editor is *not* . . .

- someone you are *not* in relationship with—not a stranger, hired hand, or fringe friend
- someone who likes to give their opinion even when you don't ask for it
- a consummate devil's advocate

A Life Editor is not something/someone you place an ad for. Finding a Life Editor is an organic process. It looks something like this:

- Spend time with people just because.
- Identify the people in your life who have the qualities and habits we've mentioned.
- Be aware of the person that rises to the surface as a potential Life Editor just by being themselves.
- Invite that person to play that role in your life. They will usually ask, "What would that require of me?" The answer is . . . "Keep doing what you're doing in my life."
- Tell the person you value them and tell them the ways they have impacted you. Help them recognize how valuable they are to you.
- Tell that person about your desire to be an Idea Mentalist.
- Continue to foster and nurture your relationship.

Finding a Life Editor shouldn't be a daunting task. You may have that person or people in your life already. It may take some time.

For years, I told my wife I wanted this kind of person in my life. I had more specific qualities I was looking for. I wanted them to be at least ten to fifteen years older than me (although this is not necessarily a requirement). I wanted them to be quirky and ask the questions an Idea Mentalist asks, like, "Who said we can't do that?" I imagined this person being an old salty-sea-dog kind of a person who occasionally cussed, questioned the status quo, broke the right rules, worked hard, and spoke in metaphor.

It took years of investing in others and sharing experiences with others to be in the fortunate place I am today with a

handful of Life Editors. People I trust. People I love. People who love me. People who help me grow.

There's Rix, the avant-garde artist, with a penchant for making people scratch their heads.

There's Len, the seasoned speaker, author, and Doctor of Semiotics, who lives on an island.

There's Tony, the medical doctor and drummer who I like to call Doctor of Drums and Friend of the Funk, who is one of the most generous souls alive.

There's David, my former "work-wife" and incredible friend, entrepreneur, artist, author, and pastor, who is not older than me but somehow cornered the market on ideas and creativity as if he were two decades my elder.

There's Michael, my best friend since fourth grade, who knows all my secrets and tells me there is nothing I could do to disappoint him.

There's Sean, my great finish-my-sentences friend, who has gone side-by-side with me through the kind of life experiences that season a relationship beyond its years—with whom I've shared more laughter and tears with in the last decade than any other friend.

There's Judi—my dear friend and mentor who breathed her last in 2021—who met with me regularly to talk art, life, relationship, God, poetry, loving humanity, and ideas. Judi's wild hair, laughter, eyes that intensely spoke, "you have my attention," and occasional creative cuss words when disapproving of something will inform me forever.

Everyone's journey to identify a Life Editor is different. There is no prescription. If you don't have one, begin imagining that person. Work towards the goal of having one. It takes spending time and investing in others yourself. It could take a good deal of time, and you'll meet wonderful people along the way.

As an Idea Mentalist, I don't know what I'd do without these people. With each of my Life Editors, I can recall specific times where they said something that altered the course of my life. My Life Editors have given me perspectives that have made me a better Idea Mentalist, but more than that, a better human.

Guerilla Cohorts

Once upon a time, the organization I worked with used to have a conference budget for upper-level staff. Conferences can be expensive. Depending on the type of conference you attend, a two-day conference with traveling expenses can cost anywhere between a couple of thousand dollars up to around $20,000. The budget for our team was somewhere around $3,000 a year per person. If you chose wisely, you maybe got to attend two conferences a year.

Twenty-ish years ago, I remember conferences being helpful for me. I would learn new ways of thinking, and I'd come back and implement new ideas. Somewhere along the line, conferences lost their luster for me, and the ROI was not there anymore. The industry was no longer helpful with very few exceptions.

I think the music industry is a good metaphor for what I feel the conference industry has become. Long ago, "making it" in the music industry (or at least the prevailing legend of the industry) was one where young artists worked in dive bars and street corners across the land—putting in hard work and long hours for little pay with the hopes of being discovered. In this world, music representatives were looking for that "new sound" and new ideas. Sure, it was a business. But it had a daring spirit. Artists were being discovered and promoted that would make you pull your car to the side of the road and say, "I've never heard this sound before."

In recent years, an artist occasionally breaks the mold and grabs our attention, but the majority seem to be run through the LA or Nashville mechanism, so they are more marketable and profitable. Yes, I am opinionated on this. I have many friends that have experienced this first-hand. And, years ago, I also sat in a record company office where I was told by two executives that I needed to make changes to my songs that fit a mold I was unwilling to fit into.

The story of today's music industry, as told by many broken and bruised artists, is one of conformity.

In a world where recording contracts are awarded on televised talent competitions, many artists have found the only way they can remain true to their daring selves and tell their story the way they want is to remain an independent artist. It's easy to record in a basement in this day and age, without someone trying to make you conform to what they want you to be. Many have found freedom and new ideas by not subscribing to the old methods.

Back to the conference industry.

My good friend and Life Editor, David, and I were at a conference one year in Chicago when we both said, "This is just not doing it anymore." David had fallen out of love with the conference scene long before me. It isn't that we thought we couldn't learn anything anymore, it was that the conference scene had become dull, undaring, and predictable. It had become a big business with profit as its heartbeat.

We made a list of the things we still loved about going to conferences . . .

. . . experiencing new cities and being exposed to new ideas
. . . experiencing new restaurants and museums, etc.

. . . sitting with our friends and tossing around ideas in cigar bars and coffee shops

. . . the freedom to speak freely when in the company of people we trust

. . . the camaraderie we felt when we were with our friends

. . . hearing from that one speaker that changed our way of thinking

. . . the break from our normal routine

. . . the hope that maybe we would come away with a golden nugget idea

That day in Chicago, an idea rose to the surface. We imagined a new kind of gathering where we weren't being marketed the conformity we were experiencing—one that captured the things we loved about getting away to a conference.

What would it look like if we . . .

. . . pooled all our team's conference resources

. . . invited all our friends to come stay with us in our city or the city of our choosing

. . . didn't charge our friends any money to attend our gathering

. . . allowed our friends to simply spend their budget on travel and lodging

. . . took our friends out to experience new restaurants in our region

. . . took our friends on field trips to places of interest

. . . hired a conversationalist/speaker to sit with us in a close-up experience

Who says we can't do that?

Our first year of trying our new idea on for size stands out in my mind as one of my favorite group experiences ever. On one winter's week in Michigan, a group of friends who wanted to become better Idea Mentalists gathered in my basement with a conversationalist/speaker we all admired. He wasn't cheap, but we had reallocated all our funding to afford him and still have money left over for an amazing experience that toppled our previous conference experiences.

Each day, the basement was full of burning candles and a food and drink spread that looked like it was prepared for the Greek gods. In the afternoon, we visited fun restaurants—one in an art gallery, one in a museum, one in a nearby college town. In the evening, we visited cigar bars, wineries, and breweries. Some mornings, we started our day with the best quirky greasy spoon restaurants in the area. Some folks stayed in our houses as opposed to a hotel.

Our speaker even agreed to do a one-day gathering we could invite our whole town to. For free.

Since that time, the term "unconferencing" has become part of the conference vernacular, and I suppose our rag tag gathering had some elements of unconferencing. Although, even unconferencing has become somewhat formulaic now.

Here's the deal . . . consider who you want to be in your Idea Mentalist cohort. Put something together. Pick the city. Pick the rules. Storyboard the gathering however you want. Assemble this gathering however you want and incorporate whatever experiences you desire. Resist the urge to spend your money on formulaic, profit-driven, cookie-cutter gatherings. Break the rules. Develop and foster relationships in a cohort. However structured or loose you prefer. And, if it doesn't work like you imagined, try something different. Just . . . don't settle.

An Idea Mentalist never settles.

Eat Meets

In the summer of 1999, I began sporadically doing a seasonal thing I call Eat Meets. Eat Meets are very simple. I tell a group of people I am meeting at a specific location at a specific time to discuss an idea with them and hear their current ideas. It's always a restaurant where we can have a good discussion. Or, a park where everyone brings their own lunch. Or a boat ride on a lake with sushi and wine.

I only invite people I think are eager to share and eager to listen. People I think can be trusted. People who have a yearning to become the best possible version of themselves. People who want to be Idea Mentalists.

The rules are simple. Get together. Eat. Drink. Talk. Period.

The only other rule is that we know why we're there. It's not simply hang time, although it is most definitely hang time. We have a goal.

The Idea Mentalist will make time to talk about ideas.

The People I Don't Know Yet

In Chapter Five of this book, "Everything New," I mentioned that saying *yes* to many things is a habit of the Idea Mentalist. Even greater than the experiences themselves, the habit of saying yes introduces you to new people. Or people you don't know well. People who have something to share and people who want you to share with them.

I can't remember what month it was when my friends Michael and Tamara Mosier approached me and asked if I had ever thought about playing the role of Santa and if I would consider playing Santa in Folsom High School's production of *Elf the Musical*. My immediate response was, "Yes." My next response was, "Let me ask my wife." My wife, Tahni agreed it would be fun and it would probably be good for me. Tahni knows I'm at my best when I get to do something creative with other people that brings joy to others.

I remember Mike and Tamara telling me, in the beginning, they thought the role would be "good for me," as well as me being good for the musical. "These students keep you young," they told me.

Something happened when I put on the Santa suit that I didn't even see coming.
Before the production even began, before I knew all the cast members, before a single actual practice, the cast asked if I'd be willing to be Santa in the homecoming parade float that traveled down Sutter Street in our Historic District in late October. That night, for the first time, Mrs. Claus painted my beard white, I stepped into red velvet pants, and cinched up a black belt around my fat suit. I didn't even have white gloves that night or my round spectacles since the production department was still acquiring some pieces of my suit. I wore my reading glasses, which sufficed. I immediately knew something magical was taking place.

As I rode in the float down Sutter Street, the looks on the faces of everyone filled my soul. Santa stands for something everyone is longing for. The smiles, the waves, the shouts, they were intoxicating. When the parade was over, I was at the end of Sutter Street. I walked back through the crowds to our restaurant. Along the way, I talked to countless children and posed for selfies and family snapshots.

I posted some photos on Facebook that evening, and immediately started getting messages from folks asking if I might consider playing Santa for parties and photo sessions.

I looked at my wife that night and said, "I'm buying a Santa suit."

The suit I wore for *Elf the Musical* belongs to the school, and I knew a Santa suit was something I needed to own. I started advertising that Santa was available and my calendar started filling up.

True confessions: In some ways, the COVID-19 troubles, old career dysfunction, and new business struggles that cast a shadow before I donned the Santa suit changed me. I didn't like parts of the person I felt I was becoming. I allowed some things to rob me of my joy. I allowed other people to rent my headspace. I battled new depths of depression. I became quicker to be frustrated. I wasn't exercising all my gifts and I wasn't doing the things that fill my soul. Self-care had gone by the wayside. The habits of the Idea Mentalist became more sporadic.

The Idea Mentalist is also human.

The Santa suit helped me regain some of the things I felt like I had lost along the way. They weren't really lost, I just hadn't been able to exercise them to the degree I longed for.

While wearing the Santa suit, the conversations with children, teachers, business owners, parents, strangers on the street, and students became a healing balm for my soul. They reanimated parts of me that were lying dormant. Santa helped me get back into the thick of it with other humans in a way I didn't see coming.

At the end of the season, I wrote Santa a letter.

> Santa, this is what I want for Christmas . . . I want everyone to feel the joy that comes from experiencing Christmas through the eyes of a child. I want everyone

to feel free to use their gifts in creative ways. I want everyone to find new joy. I want everyone to have their soul filled through relationships. I want people to pour themselves out for others. I want everyone to regain what they've lost over the last two years. I want us all to feel human again and see each other as human again. I want everyone to find rest in the busy-ness.

Sometimes, being with new people, making new friends, and deepening relationships revives parts of us that need to be revived in order to thrive. Sometimes it's those people that remind us of something that's been missing. Sometimes those new relationships surface something we never knew was there.

In the Christmas season of 2021, I spent two months and over a hundred hours with sixty high school students and a handful of faculty I had never met participating in a musical where I learned lines I didn't previously know, songs I'd never heard, and rules of engagement in an environment that was brand new to me, surrounded by people who called that theater home. After the musical was over, I spent another month meeting with over 600 students and their families in Santa gatherings at schools and private events throughout our region. I visited over twenty homes and businesses of complete strangers. How could I have known that saying yes to a musical would have me wearing a Santa suit for three months and meeting so many beautiful humans?

Those new relationships not only breathed life into my soul, they began spawning new ideas almost immediately–collaborations, gatherings, fundraisers, books, concerts, albums, and community gatherings. Many of those ideas are in the works.

The Idea Mentalist in you needs the people you don't know yet. You don't know when you'll need them. You don't know when they'll need you. So, go spend time with them.

EPILOGUE

When I shared a brief history of our restaurant, I told you the two things we would fight to defend more than anything are *experience* and *community*.

This *entire book* gets down to those two things.

Every little tidbit of information, habit, story, dare, scientific insight, history, and wisdom I've shared with you has been seeped in experience and community.

If you want to be an Idea Mentalist, experience and community must be paramount for you. If you take away anything from this book, let it be this insight.

Now, one final word . . .

I sat with my therapist once and talked about the concept of failure and the fear of failing. I've never really been afraid of failure, but there have been times in my life where I feel like I have failed.

He looked at me and chuckled, "Failure doesn't exist." I asked him to explain. I'll try to quote him:

> Failure is a construct within our own minds. It only exists because we allow it to exist as we compare ourselves to others and imagine what other people think of us. It only exists if we are more concerned with appearing to be successful to others.

We then went on to talk about experiencing more deeply, loving more, knowing more, and learning more. All of these things only come through experience and community. As we dive into experience and community, not everything will work out perfectly. Duh. We know this. But . . .

The Idea Mentalist must let go of the idea of failure.

Maybe your last idea wasn't received well.
Maybe you missed a goal.
Maybe a dream didn't work out like you planned.
Maybe your marriage ended.
Maybe you filed for bankruptcy.
Maybe your child is rebellious.
Maybe you were fired.
Maybe you lost yourself along the way.

But, did you fail? Absolutely not.

You may have changed, gained a new perspective, experienced pain and frustration, wished you would have done some things differently, lost a relationship, and/or learned some lessons.

But, you did not fail.

Fail is a four-letter word that is not becoming of an Idea Mentalist.

Idea Mentalists believe there are a plethora of ideas, options, experiences, and relationships to be explored. How could failure ever be a reality when so many new pathways exist?

You may find yourself in a tough spot right now. Wherever you are, however you feel, whatever demon you are facing, whatever is happening to you that you can't control . . . those things do not own you and they do not have permission to access your ideas. Your ideas are in a place deep inside you, free from harm, and waiting to be unleashed. They are powerful. Healing. Life-giving. Joy-inducing. You have the potential inside you for a new idea. A better idea. A life-altering idea.

If a previous experience or community let you down, I'm sorry. There are new adventures to be had and new people to meet. The world may be broken, but it is certainly not predictable or prescriptive. There are great things happening every day. Don't let your past unfortunate experience or relationships define your way forward. Unleash your Idea Mentalist and let your new success be the best silencer of the old, harmful voices.

Maybe you are in a fantastic place. You may find yourself on the precipice of a new idea. It might feel scary. Invigorating. Hopeful. You may be cautious. Maybe others are telling you to be careful. Maybe some are cheering you on. It may be a total departure from what you've known. You are on a new journey that no one will ever be able to truly experience in the way you are about to experience it. I'm excited for your future.

The world needs you. The world needs your ideas.

We can't wait to see your idea in action.

Made in the USA
Las Vegas, NV
04 January 2023